The U. S. Supreme Court is GUILTY!

Judges on trial in the "Peoples Court."
Founding The New Patriots of America,
Reclaiming our Constitutional Rights
To Let the People be Free!

Claude Wayne

ISBN 0-7414-3766-X

Published by:
INFINITY
PUBLISHING.COM
1094 New DeHaven Street, Suite 100
West Conshohocken, PA 19428-2713
Info@buybooksontheweb.com
www.buybooksontheweb.com
Toll-free (877) BUY BOOK
Local Phone (610) 941-9999
Fax (610) 941-9959

Printed in the United States of America

Printed on Recycled Paper

Published January 2007

Contents

Contents

Foreword

In all honesty I can't take full credit for writing this book. It is more the result of Divine inspiration. I have to give God credit for it. Why He choose an ordinary common sinner like me to do this is somewhat of a mystery to me. Perhaps it's because He knows I was deeply moved to the point that I wanted to start another American Revolution back in 1962 when the U.S. Supreme Court banned prayer in our public schools, and that I've been deeply outraged at many of their decisions since. He must know I lost respect for the Court when they lost respect for God. After all, the Lord can read our hearts with greater ease than we can read a book.

Regardless, I am absolutely convinced God has played the leading role in the writing of this document and its call-to-action for a Spiritual Revolution and Revival of America's religious freedoms.

I know there is a God. I have no doubt. The evidence of His intelligent design is everywhere. But to me the proof also is in the many miracles He has performed in my life. Some were small miracles. Some were large. But none have been as significant, or of greater importance than what God has revealed to me and is covered in this book. These writings are not just God's call for certain Justices (and likewise for other Federal and State Judges) to repent or leave the Court System, but for all Americans and all peoples of the world to heed to His righteousness as He pours out His Spirit upon all the earth in these critical latter times before the return of Christ.

God even gave me the title of this book. I have come to recognize those rare occasions when a thought enters my mind that is not my own to be of a spiritual nature, especially in times of asking for God's guidance. This happened in the fall of 2004. I had already written a Civil War novel which has some serious religious aspects, and I asked myself, "What should I write for my next book?" I was thinking along the lines of another novel but immediately this title popped into my head, "The U.S. Supreme Court is GUILTY!" That wasn't what I had in mind, but the more I thought about it, the more I realized it was something God was calling me to do, and it was verified by more supernatural happenings with timings that exceeded the probabilities of pure coincidence.

I started researching material and when I tried to write the book I had a terrible time condensing it into easily understood thoughts that would be interesting and have memorable impact. It was coming out as very boring legalese language. I prayed before bedtime that night in exasperation, telling God it wasn't working and asking Him to give me the right words to get these ideas across. As I was waiting to doze off, the words I would have used if I were the Defense Attorney in the case regarding prayer in the schools began to churn passionately in my mind. All of a sudden, I heard a voice in my head that was not of my origin. It wasn't my voice. It wasn't from my mind. This other voice abruptly interrupted me, saying loudly in my mind, "I Object!" I was briefly startled but calm and I thought, "And who are You?" The voice replied, "I'm the other side of the argument." As I continued to converse with the other voice, I realized God had given me a novel way to format the book and express both sides of every case regarding the court. It was a comprehensive way to cover all of the subject matter and make it more interesting for anyone to read no matter where they stand on the issues.

Soon after I started on the project, I was at my job working for a Christian owned and operated TV station in Louisville, Kentucky. Our guests on the live program were talking about bringing Judge Roy Moore to Louisville for an all day seminar. As you may recall, Judge Moore was the Chief Justice of the Alabama Supreme Court who was removed from his job by a Federal Judge for displaying a monument of the Ten Commandments. I bought tickets to the event and attended every activity, having several opportunities to talk to Judge Moore personally, and more importantly hearing what he and other officials had to say about our corrupt judiciary and decaying moral standards in America. I realized from that meeting how a few impassioned people can impact a hall full of people with the same interests, but it became very apparent to me that it's not enough to be aware of the problems; we need to get active with viable solutions on a large nationwide scale.

About that same time I was encouraged to attend a Metro Louisville Board of Aldermen meeting to consider renewal of a Gay Rights "Fairness Ordinance." At that meeting I was amazed at how deceived and ignorant some well-intentioned government officials can be regarding Christianity and the purity and sanctity of God's word. These were things God wanted to show me.

Meanwhile, the writing was progressing when I received a request from a Video Production Company to do some announcing work. I mentioned I was writing this book to one of the owners of the company and he said, "Take a look at this!" On his desk was a copy of a book just published titled, "Courting Disaster." It was actually compiled by Pat Robertson and a committee of lawyers, and is an excellent comprehensive report on the abuses of the Supreme Court. It went all the way back to decisions of the fourth Supreme Court Chief Justice, John Marshall, who was stirring Thomas Jefferson to express his concern that the court was becoming tyrannical, even back then, in its loose interpretations of the Constitution and the Bill of Rights, warping the original intent of those sacred documents and assuming powers the Court was never meant to possess. In spite of the fact that some people have criticized Pat Robertson, he is a man who has a heart for God, and his work, and the work of the lawyers who assisted in writing "Courting Disaster," is an excellent compilation of the decline of integrity in America's court system.

I purchased a copy of that book and used it to further research information for *this* book. There were many things brought out in Robertson's book regarding the judicial system in America that showed how ignorant, unjust and incompetent judges with little or no religious background can be. It kindled outrage in me. I wanted to write this book more than ever. Then the temptations of satanic forces closed in on me. I began to realize that to write it as strongly as it needs to be in order to change things, I would be subjected to intense ridicule and even get many threats. I began to ask myself, "Would it be worth it?" I had been a do-gooder several times before in my life, ran ahead of God and suffered much frustration and disappointment. I thought it would surely be a lot easier to just forget all of this, watch TV or just enjoy myself somehow. I finished Pat's book that evening and called out loud, "God! If you want me to finish writing this book You're going to have to give me a definite sign of some kind, because I'm not going to waste my time and make a fool of myself for nothing."

As I arose to go to bed I felt a strong urge in my spirit that said, "Go Outside!" I have often walked out in front of my house late at night looking up at the stars, with not even a rooftop between me and God, so I'd feel closer to Him as I prayed during stressful times in my life. So I thought, "I'll go outside and pray about this." I walked out my front door, across my front porch, turned onto my driveway and strolled down it, stopping near the street. The sky had been totally overcast all day as we had one of those gloomy all-day rains. But here, past eleven o'clock in the evening, the rain had finally stopped, yet the sky was still totally overcast.

I started to meditate and pray with my head bowed. I pleaded briefly for God to give me a sign so that I would know for sure He wanted me to continue writing on this subject. I raised my head and my arms, looked into the night sky, and I noticed the clouds had opened directly ahead of me. Then to my shock I realized the parting in the clouds was in the exact shape of a huge cross. All the rest of the sky was still totally overcast and I could see the stars through the opening. I gasped, "Oh, my God! It's a cross!" I was humbled by the realization and dropped to my knees with my arms heavenward staring at it in absolute awe, because I knew I was seeing something supernatural. The cross was perfectly perpendicular. It didn't lean left or right and the edges were perfectly straight. The most amazing thing was that those straight edges formed square corners. It was far too perfectly shaped and straight to be a random cloud formation, and it didn't move, drift apart or fade away. I realized this was God's remarkable answer to my prayer. What better sign could He give me than a sign of the cross? The only imperfection in it was on the far right edge of the crosspiece. It was somewhat fuzzy.

I kneeled there for several minutes gazing at that cross in the sky and praising God for this miracle. I said, "Thank you God! Thank You! Now I know without a doubt you want me to write the book. Yes Lord! Yes! I will write it. God, give me the right words. Guide me. Show me what to do every step of the way." I continued to gaze at the cross, almost wondering if I was dreaming. I would look away for a few seconds and then look up again. No, I wasn't dreaming. It was really there. It was truly real. I wanted to go get my camera and take a picture of it, but I realized it was too dark. God is really communicating with me, I thought. I was transfixed for several minutes and then I began to wonder why the far right edge of the cross was fuzzy. That's when the full realization of the message registered on me. God was indicating that the right side needs to be made more clear, what is correct, His righteousness. There is too much deceit and confusion in the world. Too much declaring right to be wrong and wrong to be right. <u>What is right and truly correct needs to be made more clear and sharply defined.</u>

Finally, I began to walk back in the house, and as I turned onto the porch I glanced back again at the cross to see the clouds begin to close up to an overcast sky. Yes, it was a miracle. It was supernatural for such a straight-edged perfectly shaped cross to appear at that exact moment, directly in front of me, and hold its shape for as long as it did. I continue to praise God for His miracles, and I will never forget the image of that cross in the night sky.

All of these things happened over a period of just a few weeks following several years of prayers when I was pleading with God to put some love and purpose in my life, because I felt so empty and incomplete. God has gifted me with a variety of talents and I felt I had never been able to put any of them to good use for Him, for others or for me. I was extremely frustrated and disappointed. But God heard my prayers and answered them dramatically over a short period of time. His timing is impeccable.

Acts 2: 17 says, “And it shall come to pass in the last days, saith God, I will pour out of my Spirit upon all flesh: and your sons and daughters shall prophesy, and your young men shall see visions, and your old men shall dream dreams.” I’m an old man with a dream to restore religious freedom to America. I’m certain there will be many younger men and women who will have visions to help make the dream come true.

Claude Wayne

Preface

The purpose of this book is threefold:

1. To put the majority opinions of the modern day U.S. Supreme Court on trial in the "People's Court" and prove with simple, clear and absolute truth that **the High Court is GUILTY** of being the major perpetrator of more crime, evil and ungodly degradation in America than any other governmental source, grossly lowering the bar on the Nation's moral standards. Their faulty decisions, and opinions can only be described as **enormous abuses of power and outright tyranny.** (It is important to note, however, that there are some current individual Justices and many from the past that are NOT among the accused).

2. To enlighten a long deceived, confused and complacent citizenry about the dangerous flawed reasoning and incompetence of certain Justices that is **destroying the very freedoms the First Amendment was designed to preserve.** Our government was never meant to be off-limits to God, or those who believe in God, nor should it ever be.

3. To rally the people to support an active peaceful Revolution for the Revival of our unalienable rights, founding the **New Patriots of America**, organized to boldly demand speedy judicial and social reform, restore true democracy and integrity to our republic, right the wrongs of the courts and insist our government **Let the People Be Free**!

Let me share with you one of the greatest revelations God gave me in order to write this book. We do not have to wait for judges on the Supreme Court to retire or die to restore righteous order and integrity to the court system and America at large. There is no set number of Judges for the court. **The President has the power to eliminate as well as add job positions for judges. Those Justices that are misguided and incompetent can be asked to retire or resign, and if they refuse they can be impeached.** Even though officially reducing the number of judges is a course of action that is unprecedented, it is nevertheless a

Constitutionally legal goal we can accomplish in a short period of time.

Any Judge appointed to the Court who believes the Constitution of the United States is an outdated invalid document, and that his or her personal opinion supercedes the intent and authority of the Constitution, is guilty not only of arrogant incompetence, but tyranny and gross abuse of power as well. They, in fact, are undermining the very foundation of the bench to which they have been appointed. It is Article III of the Constitution that establishes the judiciary, the Supreme Court, all subsequent courts and their jobs as Judges. Article III of the Constitution states they may keep their jobs **during good behavior.** Let me ask you: Is a lack of ability to read and understand the Constitution good behavior? NO! That's **incompetence!** Is substituting contrary personal opinions in place of lawful Constitutional purpose and intent good behavior? NO! That's adding **arrogance** to incompetence! Is turning to the laws of foreign nations as a legal basis for overturning America's laws good behavior? NO! That's tantamount to **treason!** Is not knowing the difference between right and wrong, stripping the people of their God-given unalienable sacred rights, instituting immoral standards as the law of the land against the majority will of the people good behavior? NO! That's **criminal behavior, abuse of power and outright tyranny!** And we are long overdue putting an end to it!

Here is the simple procedure by which we can end it! The Constitution gives the President the power to appoint Supreme Court Judges with the advice and consent of the Senate. Now, let's look at the situation from another perspective. The Constitution does NOT specify any number of justices for the Supreme Court. **If the President of the United States can ADD judges to the court, by the same authority and power the President can SUBTRACT judges from the court!** What is to prevent the President from simply eliminating positions on the court, or urging the retirement of, or asking for the resignation of inept or corrupt Judges on the grounds of bad behavior, and if they refuse, to signal the beginning of the impeachment process? Cutting back to 7 judges could quickly and dramatically change the majority opinion of the court to a body of Justices who respect the original intent of the Constitution to guarantee the fundamental God-given rights and freedoms of the people, forbid the government from violating these rights, and restore America as the democratic republic it was meant to be, instead of the oligarchy it has become. An oligarchy is government with final power vested in just a few. In regard to the Supreme Court, it's an **unelected** few. We must insist that the President and the Senate work together to give us a Supreme Court the majority of the people prefer, a court system **without** Judges that are guilty of bad behavior. **There is nothing more important in order to halt the moral decline of America.** The President who has the courage and integrity to make this stand for freedom and decency will be revered as great in American history. If our current President doesn't have what it takes to accomplish this, then we must campaign to elect one who will.

The only way we, the American People, can regain our rights is to **boldly stand our ground** and **insist that absolutely NO ONE, Supreme Court Judge or whoever, is going to be allowed to deny us our God-given Constitutional rights. We must make our voices heard by our elected representatives, let them know ENOUGH IS ENOUGH and we're not going to put up with this gross injustice and tyranny any longer. We have to motivate them to act to protect our freedom of beliefs and human rights or face enormous, determined and organized opposition at the polls, because as long as we are quiet and complacent politicians will never act on our behalf.**

Everyone needs to know the truth about the corruption that has taken place in the dark shadows of our ignorance and complacency. For far too long we have allowed Supreme Court Judges to gradually and **illegally set themselves up as sovereign dictatorial gods to rule over us**, seemingly leaving little recourse for the majority will of the people to prevail. **But prevail we can, and must, in order to be free!** We cannot continue to let America morph into an ever-degrading oligarchy with a corrupt court system that has abused its authority by overruling the Constitution, the will of the People, the power of the Congress and The Executive Branch, usurping the rightful heritage the Framers of our government provided for us. Today's out-of-order court is NOT how our government was meant to be, nor should remain to be.

This book will shed light on this tyranny and provide a plan of immediate action to exercise checks and balances to restore true democracy to our Nation, and let the majority will of the People rule in respect to erroneous judicial decisions of the courts regarding Separation of Church and State, Creationism versus Evolution, Abortion, Perverse Sexual Conduct and Same-Sex Marriage, Hate Crimes, Legal Protection of Pornography, Criminal Rights and other issues. Getting the court system back on track will destroy the ACLU, Americans United for Separation of Church and State, and other such evil organizational affronts to Godly moral values. We can and must SAVE the Court, the Government, and most of all the Fundamental Freedoms and Rights of the People, as designed by the inspired will and wisdom of the Founding Fathers of America, which are set forth in the Declaration of Independence and the Constitution of the United States. **Let us uphold those sacred values and birth a new wave of patriotism that will take America back to its original glory as a nation under God.**

America has never been closer to being destroyed from within. Too many fought and died to protect our freedoms from foreign enemies to let our rights and liberties be destroyed by disillusioned, incompetent, unqualified officials within our own government. This is more than just a cultural war. It's not just Conservatives against Liberals, or Republicans against Democrats. It's a battle of Good versus Evil, God versus Satan. Whether we like it or not, we battle NOT against flesh and blood but against evil principalities and powers. We're engaged in **an all-out Spiritual War** for the hearts, souls and minds of all mankind. It's a war more threatening, more dangerous and more important than any war America has ever fought, because it's a war that personally affects us all, a war where the battleground is the mind, soul and spirit of every person. The opinion of each citizen is an important deciding part of the conflict. No one is exempt. There is no neutral ground. God makes it clear that if you are not for Him you are already against Him. We cannot serve two masters. We will love one and hate the other. As it stands, so-called liberal forces pulling strongly off-track to the left have derailed the original sacred central ideals of America, and now make us a nation divided against itself. This is a serious situation because Christ himself said, "A house divided against itself cannot stand."

So we must set the example for unity and become **New Patriots of America.** Like the original Patriots who founded this

Country, we must be diligent, devoted and dedicated to the cause of a government **protecting, not rejecting** our rightful freedoms. We must wage a **New American Revolution to revive our very basic God-given rights and freedoms with a goal NOT to condemn people, but to defend principles.** We must impress upon every branch of government that they must respect the principles of freedom, morality and rights for us all.

We will not fight this war alone. We will not fight with weapons that bring death, but with the weapon that brings life: the power of the word. **With faith in God's Word and His righteousness, He promises we will surely be victorious when we pray and seek His face.** Like the Patriots who founded America, let's turn to God asking for His guidance, His Wisdom and His blessings in the cause of reviving America as it started, as a Judeo-Christian nation, yet respecting everyone's free will and beliefs. Let us pray and stand up for the cause of Freedom of Religion, Freedom of Speech, Freedom of the Press, and most importantly, Freedom from government interference with our rights as human beings, and all other liberties intended by the Constitution, recognizing God as the Supreme authority over our lives and our nation. **Let the Revolution begin! Let the New Patriots of America march forward with a Revival of our God-given unalienable rights. And let the people be Free!**

Chapter 1

The Arraignment: Defining Crimes against the People's Freedoms

This literary trial, on behalf of the majority will of the People of the United States, focuses on **those Justices of the United States Supreme Court** who have ruled against the purpose and intent of the rights and freedoms guaranteed to the people by the U.S. Constitution, which these judges have sworn to uphold, and **charges them with Incompetence, Treason, Abuse of Power and Tyranny,** crimes to which they would surely plead not guilty. We will clearly prove the fallacies of their reasoning. Lets start by defining true freedom.

> *All citizens in a democratic republic shall have the right to freely think for themselves, to reach conclusions, to have opinions, to believe and worship God as they see fit, even freedom to the extent of not believing or worshiping, all with total impunity.*
>
> *And all citizens have the right to freely and openly express their opinions and beliefs both privately and publicly, including in all chambers of Government, with no legal Governmental censorship, restriction or punishment of the free expression of thought in speech or the printed word.*
>
> *The Government shall not establish an official State religion and force the people to practice it exclusively, to the exclusion of all other beliefs, and no branch of government shall interfere with, restrict, violate or prohibit the free exercise of religion.*
>
> *In a truly free society the Government shall not abridge the right of the people to peaceably assemble and petition the Government for a redress of grievances.*

The preceding is a **common sense understanding** of the **intent** of the First Amendment to the Constitution of the United States. Because the King of England established the "Church of England" and forced the people to exclusively attend it for worship, the authors of the Bill of Rights added to the U. S. Constitution the First Amendment to specifically prevent the U.S. Government from establishing a "Church of America" as the only church the people could attend, which would deny their right and freedom to believe as they see fit.

In other words, the **purpose of the First Amendment is to restrict only the government** in order to **Let the People be FREE!** The Supreme Court fails to recognize that **as a major part of government even the courts are restricted from interfering in any way with the free exercise of religion or any other Constitutional rights of the people.** After all, government of the people, by the people and for the people means the final authority of rule rests with the people. That's Democracy! That's TRUE Freedom! We the People, created the government to serve us, not to oppress us and enslave us to make us bow to the will of a non-elected few. Now, let's review what the First Amendment actually states as written:

Congress shall make no law respecting an establishment of religion, or prohibiting the free exercise thereof; or abridging the freedom of speech, or of the press, or the right of the people peaceably to assemble, and to petition the Government for a redress of grievances.

That's it! That is every word of the First Amendment in its entirety, as it was written, ratified and added to the Constitution, and has been in force since December 15, 1791. Nothing more. Nothing less. That is the actual law of the Constitution and the only legally written portion of it making reference to a relationship between religion and the government.

The First Amendment in NO way guarantees separation of Church and State. It's not about separation. It's not about establishment. It's all about FREEDOM! It's about guaranteeing the most basic, most important and most sacred rights we have as human beings. That's why they made it the First Amendment. It guarantees all citizens absolute Freedom of Religion, Freedom of Speech, Freedom of the Press and

peaceful assembly for a redress of grievances, on every inch of American soil including all government properties. And the highly misunderstood "establishment clause" is a restriction only on government to not violate our rights and let the people be free.

Former President Ronald Reagan put it this way, "I just want to point out, the first amendment of the Constitution was not written to protect the people of this country from religious values. It was written to protect religious values from government tyranny!"

So, regarding the infamous case of Engel vs. Vitale brought before the Supreme Court that resulted in the banning of prayer in America's public schools in 1962, the Court should have looked at the First Amendment and asked themselves, "Did Congress make a law regarding the establishment of religion?" No! **Congress** made no law. Any further judgment beyond that was not in compliance to Constitutional law, but rather the personal opinions of the Justices of the Court. At that point, they would have been justified to refuse to hear the case, but instead they went far beyond their jurisdictional powers to assume their opinions superceded the purpose and intent of the written Constitutional law.

"I Object! I demand to be heard!"

And who are you Sir, to suddenly appear in this literary People's Court?

"I represent those on the Other Side Of The Argument. You may hereafter refer to me as 'Mr. Other Side,' and in the interest of legal representation under the law, I demand that you allow me to define freedom and serve as counsel to defend the court's rulings. I am a gay evolutionist and member of the BAR (Bold Atheists Roundtable). Most all of my views are supported by the American Civil Liberties Union (ACLU), and by decisions of the Supreme Court of the United States. Who could be better qualified to defend today's modern court? I have a Master's in matters of law and court procedures. And I want to know by what authority you claim to be an expert critic on matters of the law and the judgments set forth in America's courts?"

Before I answer your question Mr. Other Side, I would like to state that as a common sense American citizen you may henceforth refer to me as 'Mr. Common Sense.' I accept your offer to present a different, or even a totally opposite argument, to define freedom and defend the Court. Like those who established this nation, I believe in an Almighty Creator. It is by belief in His authority and fundamental Judeo-Christian principles that the Founding Fathers of America directed their will and patterns of thought to literally construct the Declaration of Independence and the Constitution of the United States, which are the absolute central pillars and legal foundations establishing this nation's Federal Government.

Mr. OTHER SIDE: I must say you make a minor point, but in my opinion you make no sense, Mr. Common Sense. It is highly irregular to put a court on trial in a book, especially the highest court in America. How can you adhere to normal court procedure? Who is the judge? And where is the jury?

Mr. COMMON SENSE: The readers of this book will serve as both the judge and jury to decide on the guilt or innocence of certain Justices of the Supreme Court and various judges of the Federal Circuit Courts. The procedure will not hinge on normal court decorum, but will be more of a conversational presentation of facts to reach a truthful accusation of charges against the defendants, somewhat similar to that of a Grand Jury.

Mr. OTHER SIDE: I must say this is most unusual, but before we proceed, allow me to remind you that you have not answered the question of *YOUR* credentials to be respected as an expert on the subject of law and the interpretation thereof. Have you been to Law School? Did you pass the BAR Exam? Are you a practicing and outstanding lawyer in whom anyone could have faith to present a credible legal argument?

Mr. COMMON SENSE: I find it interesting that an atheist would mention faith while questioning someone's credentials. No Sir, I have not been to Law School, but I can read and think, and I have the ability to understand the purpose and intent of the laws and those who make the laws. You see, Sir, I do not have to be a professional or expert in the fields of architecture or engineering to see that the Tower of Pisa is leaning. Likewise, I do not have to be a professional expert lawyer to see that something is crooked and so completely out of line, (such as the decisions of some Supreme Court Justices) that it sticks out like a sore thumb for all to see. Even a child, or the least educated among us, can tell when something is enormously crooked or biased too far to one side.

Mr. OTHER SIDE: I find it disgusting that you mentioned a so-called God as the central pillar supporting the foundation of America. You know I'm an atheist, yet you have the audacity to believe God exists. I'm greatly offended by your belief. That's why the Supreme Court has declared expression of your belief to be wrong and unconstitutional. **You have no right to offend me.** I demand and defend the legal precedent that the law should protect me from your offensive opinion. What do you say to that, Mr. Common Sense?

Mr. COMMON SENSE: I say to you the same thing the Justices of the Supreme Court should have said to Steven Engel and Madalyn Murray O'Hair, that it is your privilege to be offended. That's every citizen's right. In a free society, common sense tells us we must respect the freedom of others to have a difference of opinion. However, having an opinion should never be a punishable crime. It's only natural that a person is offended by things with which they disagree. But **being offended, in and of itself, is no reason for legal judgment to be granted in your favor.** If being offended became the legal basis upon which court cases rest, then every court case in history would have to be reversed, because the losing party in a court ruling is always offended. I have done you no harm because I believe something different, or even totally contrary to your beliefs. You still have the right to believe as you see fit with complete impunity, yet you desire to deprive me of my right to believe as I see fit. What kind of equality under the law is that? If anything, I have more of a right to be offended by your belief than you do of mine, because my belief is based on God's truths and yours is based on lies, misconceptions and falsehoods.

Mr. OTHER SIDE: Objection! There's no proof there is a God, but there's plenty of proof that we are the result of millions of years of evolution. It's been taught in America's schools for many years by teachers from pre-school to the highest levels of education in our colleges and universities, because it's been proven to a be a fact by some of the most respected scientists, archaeologists, paleontologists and anthropologists on the planet.

Mr. COMMON SENSE: I beg to differ, Mr. Other Side. **Evolution has never been proven to be a fact. It is only a theory**, although it has been mistakenly taught in our schools as fact. I will offer our jury of readers a compelling argument revealing that evolution is more the product of fantasy than fact a little later. But first I want to point out how naive you are, Mr. Other Side, to not recognize the most compelling and obvious evidence before us, that **your very existence is proof there is a God.** You and I are both created in the image of God. He breathed into man His spirit that has the ability to love and hate. We have the ability to see and hear, smell, taste and feel. We have the power of mobility. But most of all we have the ability to think and reason for ourselves. We have a free will. These are among the many characteristics that reflect God's image in us.

Mr. OTHER SIDE: Foolishness! That's pure foolishness, I say. Just your opinion against mine. You offer no real proof. Just hearsay.

Mr. COMMON SENSE: My dear Mr. Other Side, do you want to go on record as saying that your very existence is a matter of hearsay?

Mr. OTHER SIDE: No. I want to go on record as saying my existence is the result of millions of years of the evolutionary progression to perfection.

Mr. COMMON SENSE: Would you agree, Sir, that truth is the evidence of undisputable fact?

Mr. OTHER SIDE: Only **if it agrees with my opinion!**

Mr. COMMON SENSE: Even accepting that limitation on understanding truth, denying the truth does not make the truth go away, anymore than an ostrich causes the danger of a fearful predator to disappear by sticking it's head in the sand. In other words, blinding oneself to the truth doesn't change the facts.

Mr. OTHER SIDE: And the simple fact is.. there is no God. That is my idea of truth, and the Supreme Court is justified in keeping the government neutral on the matter, forcing everyone else to do the same to keep government separate from religion. This is equitable justice. And everyone knows that Justice is blind! It's etched in stone.

Mr. COMMON SENSE: At last, we have something we can agree on. Justice should be blind in regard to equal application of the law. **Yes, Justice is blind, but Judges should not be.** So this is a good time to explain what I mean by Common Sense Logic as it relates to the law. **A Common Sense application of the law takes into consideration all and every piece of evidence relating to the case on trial.** Do you agree with that, Mr. Other Side?

Mr. OTHER SIDE: Absolutely not! In fact, I believe just the opposite. In order to achieve purity of justice, I believe it is necessary to **reduce all thought to a finite indisputable point.**

Mr. COMMON SENSE: That's like looking at part of a sentence in the Constitution with a magnifying glass and ignoring the rest of the clause because the glass is not focused on it. (which is what the Supreme Court did in regards to the "establishment" and "freedom of Religion" clauses of the First Amendment). I conclude then, that your reasoning, **like some Supreme Court Justices**, is based on a narrow-minded viewpoint that excludes all facts outside a small point of focus, while common sense is more broad-minded, ignoring no evidence or facts.

Mr. OTHER SIDE: I wouldn't put it that way, but I suppose we all have a right to our opinions, don't we? You wouldn't deny me that right, would you?

Mr. COMMON SENSE: An excellent point, Mr. Other Side, which brings us back to the case being presented when you arrived. The Court should have respected the unalienable right of every person to have an opinion without being restricted or punished for it. It's just common sense that freedom, as originally defined in the beginning of this book, gives every citizen the right to freely think for themselves, to reach conclusions, to have opinions and to worship God as they see fit, even freedom to the extent of not believing or acknowledging God. Every human being has the right to freely and openly express their opinions and beliefs both privately and publicly, even in all chambers of government. Free people must be allowed these rights with total and complete impunity.

Mr. OTHER SIDE: Let me point out that the 1962 case you were alluding to was not a case of the free expression of beliefs, because it was a matter involving a man's son of a different religion than the composers of the prayer, who was being forced to recite that prayer written by a public school board and led by an adult teacher. Therefore, it was a case of a school board, which was supported by Federal funding, acknowledging God. That constitutes a department of the Federal government acting in the capacity of establishing religion. An act clearly prohibited by the first sentence of the First Amendment of the Constitution. Children shouldn't have their minds shaped by the religious beliefs of a school board or a teacher before the age when they can think and reason for themselves.

Mr. COMMON SENSE: I beg to differ on that. Children can and do think and reason for themselves. As human beings we can't help it. It's the natural result of having a brain. How else could they learn anything? They are still free to think for themselves and make decisions. Try to feed a baby something it doesn't like and it will spit it out.

Mr. OTHER SIDE: You miss the point, Mr. Common Sense. Parents shouldn't have to tolerate a school board or a teacher prejudicing their child by forcing things into their brains that the parents oppose. Steven Engel was a member of a religion other than Christianity. He had a right to oppose a representative of the government (and that's what a public school teacher is) forcing doctrine or action on his child that he opposes as contrary to his beliefs, such as the clasping of hands and bowing of the head. He stated, "That's not the way we pray."

Mr. COMMON SENSE: There was no doctrine being forced on the child other than a mere acknowledgement of God and asking for his blessing. Hardly something that could be considered harmful in any way. The prayer was voluntary. The children were encouraged to recite a simple prayer, NOT FORCED. Mr. Engel's son could have kept his mouth shut or looked out the window if he wanted to and not participated. This is clearly a case of religious intolerance.

Mr. OTHER SIDE: Mr. Common Sense, please, **use a little common sense,** will you? We both know children's minds are like clay waiting to be shaped by those in authority over them. They're inclined to do what they're told to do and become prejudiced with religious beliefs. And that was why the case was brought to court. He didn't want his child taught things he didn't believe in. For instance, Madalyn Murray O'Hair, an atheist, had a right to not want her son exposed to a lot of phony baloney from the bible.

Mr. COMMON SENSE: I would like to point out that religious beliefs represent the highest ethical standards of humanity. And to deny that they can be passed from one generation to the next in school means that our children will learn only what is left, lower ethical standards or none. All this time, since the 1962 banning of prayer in schools by the Supreme Court, the vast majority of parents had their children taught some ungodly things they didn't believe in. Because the Supreme Court Justices weren't broad-minded enough, and didn't have the common sense to see the dangers of banning God's moral principles in the classroom, our schools have produced a continuously degenerating society to where today the biggest concerns are children carrying weapons to school, shooting one another, illicit sex, unwanted pregnancies leading to abortions, drug and alcohol abuse, grand theft to support a drug habit, insubordination, rebellion, confusion, feelings of rejection and suicide, just to name a few. Compare that to the biggest problems prior to 1962 such as being tardy, cheating on tests, not doing homework, chewing gum or talking in class without permission. I hereby state **the U.S. Supreme Court is GUILTY of contributing to the delinquency of millions of minors in America.** What's worse is that there were many generations of them that grew to adulthood exposed to a lower standard of ethics and scholastic achievement leading to a higher adult crime rate.

Mr. OTHER SIDE: That's a rather harsh accusation, isn't it? After all, the Supreme Court Justices were just doing their job to the best of their ability. You can't hold them responsible of being guilty of a crime. That's unheard of. Besides, in a society of pluralistic beliefs, religion is best kept out of the public arena and taught to children privately at home or in the church or temple.

Mr. COMMON SENSE: We're not talking about the State teaching religion by a prayer that simply acknowledges God and asks for His blessing. For the record, this was the prayer in it's entirety, *"Almighty God, we acknowledge our dependence on Thee, and we beg Thy blessings upon us, our parents, our teachers and our country."* What terrible harm could come from that?

Mr. OTHER SIDE: First of all, in my opinion, acknowledging God is teaching children a falsehood, and has no place in a public classroom. The Supreme Court acted properly to ban the school board from enforcing the recital of such rubbish and making it unconstitutional.

Mr. COMMON SENSE: Again, your narrow-minded reasoning, which I'll admit coincides with the majority of Supreme Court Justices of that time, is beginning to be as obviously out of line as the Leaning Tower of Pisa. A public school board is not a law-making body of the government, and certainly not the Congress of the United States, which is the specific body of government the Constitution prohibits from making a law respecting an establishment of religion. They completely misinterpreted the intent of the First Amendment to mean it guarantees separation of Church and State, when in fact it prohibits the government from violating everyone's right to freedom of religion, freedom of speech, freedom of the press and the right to peaceful assembly. Of course, common sense logic suggests that the Supreme Court has a duty to defend the actual written Constitutional law, not to re-invent it by substituting contrary personal opinions.

Mr. OTHER SIDE: Wrong, Mr. Common Sense! Please note that the Constitution gives the Supreme Court the right to interpret the Constitution and the laws under its jurisdiction. Therefore the **personal opinions** of the Justices are valid and final in all trials.

Mr. COMMON SENSE: I will have to admit that is a common misconception, Mr. Other Side. Article three of the Constitution establishes the Supreme Court and its judicial powers. Nowhere in the wording does the Constitution give Supreme Court Judges the power to "interpret" the Constitution. It "extends**"** judicial powers to them. It only follows logically that a Supreme Court Judge must uphold the written Constitutional law. The Judge can magnify or extend the intent of the law, but absolutely does **not** have the authority to make a ruling that is **contrary to the intent and purpose of the written law**. A Judge who has the arrogance to substitute contrary personal opinions, or the ignorance to rule against the written wording of the Constitution, such as ignoring the phrase "prohibiting the free exercise thereof," is GUILTY of contempt of the Constitution, the Law of the Land, the Founders of our Nation (who composed the Constitution) and the sacred Creator-endowed unalienable rights they valued, the same cherished liberties millions of American warriors have so valiantly fought and died for since this nation was founded. **The Contemporary U. S. Supreme Court is GUILTY of contempt for the highest ideals America has ever embodied.**

Mr. OTHER SIDE: Strong words, Mr. Common Sense! But what do you have to back them up? I believe it's still a matter of your word against the court's word, just your opinion against theirs. What makes you think your opinion is any better than ours? I'd say that makes us even. It's an equal draw with nothing to tip the legal scale one way or the other. That is, until you consider the fact that the Supreme Court has already ruled in favor of my side of the argument. That **makes <u>complete</u> 'Separation of Church and State' the law of the land** and there's nothing you can do about it.

Mr. COMMON SENSE: I can **prove** Separation of Church and State is the most misunderstood line of reasoning ever used by Judges of the Courts and pawned off on the American People as the purpose and intent of the First Amendment. Look at it again.

"*Congress shall make no law respecting the establishment of religion, or prohibiting the free exercise thereof.*" Is the phrase "Separation of Church and State" anywhere among those words? Obviously not. Yet if you were to ask most Americans if the first Amendment guarantees separation of Church and State they mistakenly would say, "yes, it does!" Let the record show this true fact: **The written law of the Constitution does <u>NOT</u> guarantee separation of Church and State. The original intent was to guarantee freedom from government interference with the free exercise of religion.**

Mr. OTHER SIDE: A point of little value, since the Courts and most of the people readily recognize "separation" to be the true meaning of the First Amendment, regardless.

Mr. COMMON SENSE: Of little value? **Is a lie equal to the truth?** Let me shed some light on why so many people, even lawyers and Justices of the high court, mistakenly and loosely conclude that "separation" is the <u>legal intent</u> of Constitutional law.

Mr. OTHER SIDE: Go ahead. Make a fool of yourself. You'll never be able to convince anyone. Their minds are already made up by years of believing separation is a good thing.

Mr. COMMON SENSE: To a degree you may be right. Dr. William James, known as the "Father of Modern Psychology" once stated, "There is nothing so absurd but if you repeat it often enough people will believe it." Nevertheless, I must reveal the truth. The phrase was first penned by Thomas Jefferson in a letter written to the Danbury Baptist Association of Connecticut. The Danbury Baptists were concerned about a rumor that another religious group, the Congregationalists, were going to be declared America's national religion. Part of Jefferson's letter to the Baptists stated, "*Believing with you that religion is a matter which lies solely between man and his God, that he owes account to none other for his faith or his worship, that the legitimate powers of government reach actions only, and not opinions, I contemplate with sovereign reverence that the act of the whole American people which declared that their legislature should make no law respecting the establishment of religion, or prohibiting the free exercise thereof, thus building a wall of separation between church and state.*"

Jefferson's intent was to assure the Danbury Baptists that the government was walled-in (held back) from making any law establishing an official State religion, or dictating how the people were or were not to worship God. **Let the record show that Thomas Jefferson was NOT implying anything about a wall completely separating church and state.** Yet, due to the ignorance of Justice Hugo Black, it has been loosely and mistakenly quoted since 1962 as an alternate interpretation for the meaning of the first sentence in the First Amendment. Unthinking or crafty lawyers, the ACLU, Judges and the public have erroneously misunderstood it, or intentionally misused it to mean an actual and complete separation of church and state.

Mr. OTHER SIDE: I would say, they correctly understood it to be a guaranteed truth.

Mr. COMMON SENSE: Let me get this straight. Are you willing to go on record to say the First Amendment clearly implies a **total and complete** separation of Church and State?

Mr. OTHER SIDE: I don't have to go on record. The Supreme Court has already declared it many times, such as Justice Hugo Black's clarification on the matter in his writing of the majority six-to-one decision in the 1962 case of Engle vs. Vitale that stated,

"In this country, it is no part of the business of government to compose official prayers for any group of the American people to recite as part of a religious program carried on by government... By the time of the adoption of the Constitution, our history shows that there was a widespread awareness among many Americans of the dangers of a union of Church and State."

Mr. COMMON SENSE: That's where Justice Black was dead wrong. There **never was any concern** on the part of the Founders of this nation about dangers of a union of Church and State. They just didn't want the State to control the church, but respected the principle that the Church had every right and responsibility to be totally free to rule over, take part in, and control the Government. To say that the State has no right whatsoever to be involved in the affairs of the church, and that the church has no right to be involved in the affairs of state would be like saying a person's head should have no interconnection with their body because they are two different entities designed to perform separate functions. **To continue to say the Constitution guarantees separation of Church and State, instead of what it actually says and means, is to pave the way for the moral beheading of American culture and society.** The Founders of America were wise enough to know there must be a reciprocal and mutual correlation between Church and State. They recognized that God and the Bible (the guidebook of God) were the highest authority over the people and their government. They respected God's law as the supreme law of the land, not the personal prejudices or ignorance of Supreme Court judges. Perhaps the word "Supreme" went to the heads of some of those Justices who thought they were supposed to be the supreme authority over America. But it was never meant to be that way. Study the lives and beliefs of those men who constructed the foundations of this nation. Their respect of authority followed this order: God first, then the Bible, the People, the Congress, the Executive Branch and then the Supreme Court. The Court was regarded as the last line of authority and was expected to hold the order together, not reverse it.

Mr. OTHER SIDE: That's another ridiculous statement. The government should never be used as a vessel to express religious ideology. **Separation of Church and State makes us a free society by preventing one person or religion from forcing their**

beliefs on another person or religion, or those of us who believe in no religion.

Mr. COMMON SENSE: Religion is the total embodiment of the highest ideals of mankind. It reflects our deepest, most sacred and important ideologies that touch and inspire the entirety of our total being, that is body, soul and spirit. Don't you see this Mr. Other Side?

Mr. OTHER SIDE: Don't make me laugh. I have no religion. I believe in none of that trash. I believe the Supreme Court has acted wisely to protect me and people of faiths other than that of yours from your fanatical, radical ideas and practices.

Mr. COMMON SENSE: You have a religion, Mr. Other Side. Religion is simply defined as what a person believes and practices in regard to God. You're an atheist. You believe there is no God. So atheism is your religion. Granted, it's the simplest and cheapest religion. You're never expected to make a donation of any kind, but atheism is your religion. It's your belief regarding God.

Mr. OTHER SIDE: Ha. Ha. Very funny Common Sense, Old Pal. The funniest part is how you twist words around to say *no* religion *is r*eligion. How absurd.

Mr. COMMON SENSE: What's absurd in all of this is that the misconception regarding separation of Church and State, if taken to mean an absolute and total dissection, will mean not only that the Ten Commandments could never be displayed on Government property, it would mean that we would have to remove "In God we Trust" from our currency, and not say "Under God" in the Pledge of Allegiance.

Mr. OTHER SIDE: What's the big deal? It's only words. What difference does it make?

Mr. COMMON SENSE: Words make a big difference in how we think and what we regard as truth, how we value various aspects of life and even the outcome of court trials. But there's a greater danger to falsely believing in the myth of complete Separation of Church and State. If this is fully applied as an axiom of law, it will mean the Post Office could be prevented from delivering mail to churches, synagogues, temples or any organization or person affiliated with religion. It could be argued that Bibles have no place in a court of law for a declaration of truth. There are many more ridiculous "separations" that could be brought to trial, but the most serious is that **some anti-religious maniac or organization, with support from the ACLU, could demand that people who go to a church must register as church members and <u>cannot be registered to vote in government elections</u>.** If we're to have PURE and COMPLETE Separation of Church and State politicians will have to dump out of their heads every high ideal, spark of wisdom and morality relating to religious beliefs in order to run for, or hold public office. (Although I'll admit there have been some politicians who seemed to have done just that). **Of course, the comeback for people of faith would be that if they are denied a right to vote, they shouldn't have to pay taxes either.** Do you think that's what the authors of the Constitution intended the First Amendment to mean? See how absurd Separation of Church and State can be? <u>Belief in "Separation Thinking" is a separation from wisdom</u>.

Mr. OTHER SIDE: Separation may do more to improve society than anything. At least, it would put an end to all of the religious bickering that interferes with the affairs of State. Besides, it doesn't matter what the founding fathers intended. We have a right to re-think and change the Constitution to suit today's more modern way of thinking.

Mr. COMMON SENSE: The Constitution can only be legally changed with the consent of the people by legal amendment. Activist judges changing it by inserting their personal prejudices is **tyranny**! But think about this. Since atheism is a religious belief, even you could be prevented from voting. Why are you so opposed to God and those who wish to worship Him, to treasure His blessings, protection, mercy, forgiveness, salvation, and most of all His eternal love?

Mr. OTHER SIDE: It rubs me the wrong way. And so do you. I repeat, you have no right to push your religion off on me or anyone. There are things about your belief in that so-called Good Book of yours that need to be declared hate crimes, like derogatory remarks about homosexuals and such. Your kind need to be silenced by the sound judgment of our Justices of Law from proselytizing the hatreds in your religion.

Mr. COMMON SENSE: What right do you, homosexuals, judges or anyone have to silence the word of God or declare it a hate book? No one, and no free government, has the right to silence anyone's beliefs and their right to express them. We need free speech. You and your liberal-minded friends always demand tolerance of your lifestyles and beliefs, but I would like to point out you are never tolerant and show great hatred in respect to the beliefs of others who differ with you. Where is your love and tolerance? And I would further like to state that if the government would legislate a hate law, or the court should rule in that direction, that law or decision would be a hate crime in itself. It would be hatred for the righteousness of God and those who uphold His laws. It's a sign of maturity to be tolerant, to love and have concern for others who have different perspectives and opinions regarding what life is all about, but it can't be a one-way street. We all need to be tolerant enough to exchange ideals. How else will we be able to grow, expand our minds to greater levels of understanding, to appreciate and learn to love one another in spite of our differences? If you have confidence that your philosophies of life are so substantial and correct, you should be glad to share them with the rest of humanity, and be confident your principles are sound enough to stand up to criticism. Could it be you lack conviction in your beliefs, Mr. Other Side? Is that why you feel I'm rubbing you the wrong way?

Mr. OTHER SIDE: I'll have conviction soon enough, when I see you're convicted of treason for criticizing the High Court of America before this jury of readers. I will continue to defend the U. S. Supreme Court and all modern-thinking activist judges, and prove their decisions are right and just.

Mr. COMMON SENSE: On that challenge, let us adjourn this session of legal and social arguments. Prepare your defense, Mr. Other Side, because I'm prepared to defend the Constitution of the United States and the ethics of the men who wrote it, to prove those who circumvent it to be GUILTY .

This Session of The People's Literary Court is adjourned until the next Chapter.

Chapter 2

Origins of Authority & Law

The People's Court is now in order for the 2nd Session in the trial of The People Vs. Supreme Court Decisions.

Mr. COMMON SENSE: Since I led off with the first Session of this trial I respectfully yield to you starting this session, Mr. Other Side. You may begin the questioning.

Mr. OTHER SIDE: I return to the original argument at hand, the establishment of authority. I'm not satisfied you answered this question— By what authority can you claim to challenge the workings, rulings and authority of the duly appointed Justices of the Supreme Court?

Mr. COMMON SENSE: By the same authority respected by the original Founders of America, such men as George Washington, Thomas Jefferson, Benjamin Franklin, Alexander Hamilton, Samuel Adams, John Adams, John Hancock, James Madison and all of those who contributed to the founding and signing of the Constitution into legal existence. **They owe no one an apology for their belief in the Judeo-Christian laws of God upon which the Constitution was based.**

Mr. OTHER SIDE: There you go again, offending me with your insinuation there is a God.

Mr. COMMON SENSE: It's not an insinuation. It's an outright declaration of the truth. You shall know the truth. And the truth will set you free.

Mr. OTHER SIDE: Don't toss those Christian quotes around. It has no meaning to me, and no legal bearing upon the various aspects of the case before this jury of readers.

Mr. COMMON SENSE: On the contrary, Sir. It has a profound bearing upon all cases before all courts. Mr. Other Side, I believe you just revealed a weakness in your defense that reflects the same weakness of your client, the Supreme Court, namely that the whole truth is of little consequence in decisions made regarding the intent of the law because of a social agenda to warp or ignore the original standards of social culture and foundations of American justice. This nation was founded by men whose faith in Judeo-Christian beliefs as outlined in the Bible influenced every aspect of the establishment of this country and the laws by which we are governed.

Mr. OTHER SIDE: There is no evidence to support that frivolous claim. No laws or nothing in the Constitution makes any reference to America being established as a Christian nation. In fact, the First Amendment indicates just the opposite, making it clear the government can establish NO religion. So where's your proof?

Mr. COMMON SENSE: The establishment clause was a restriction on the government to not establish any one Christian denomination as an official state religion. But proof that America was established as a Christian nation is in our historic record, revealing the beliefs and character of the men who wrote the Declaration of Independence and the Constitution as well as laws of Congress. During the Constitutional Convention of 1787 when the delegates were deadlocked over how to form the new government Benjamin Franklin said, *"I have lived, Sir, a long time, and the longer I live, the more convincing proofs I see of this truth: That God governs in the affairs of man. And if a sparrow cannot fall to the ground without His notice, is it probable that an empire can rise without His aid."* Franklin called for prayer, after which the contention between delegates eased and the details of our Constitution came together. Author and Historian of American history, David Barton has done extensive research and written many books and documents on the religious heritage of America. In his video and audio transcript titled, "America's Godly Heritage" he notes Biblical concepts that influenced the composition of the Constitution. For example, the concept for the three branches of our government are outlined in Isaiah 33:22; the principle behind the separation of powers was based on Jeremiah 17:9; the basis of tax exemptions for churches was found in Ezra 7:24. Want more proof of our Christian heritage?

Mr. OTHER SIDE: No. Thank you! Please spare me!

Mr. COMMON SENSE: I'm trying to spare you, and our jury of readers, the embarrassment and dangers of ignorance. In his address to the military October 11, 1798 John Adams stated, *"Our Constitution was made only for a moral and religious people. It is wholly inadequate for the government of any other."* I quote Thomas Jefferson's notes on Virginia dated 1782 in which he wrote, *"Can the liberties of a nation be thought secure when we have removed their only firm basis, a conviction in the minds of the people that these liberties are of the Gift of God?"* In a letter to his daughter, Betsy, dated August 20, 1796 Patrick Henry stated, *"I think religion of infinitely higher importance than politics."* Noah Webster said, *"No truth is more evident to my mind than that the Christian religion must be the basis of any government intended to secure the rights and privileges of a free people."* I could fill a book with such quotes. These are only a few examples of the role of the Judeo-Christian values revered by early Americans and Founders of this country.

Mr. OTHER SIDE: What makes you think those so called Judeo-Christian beliefs are the only beliefs by which we should live? There are many different religious beliefs in the world, even no religious beliefs by some, such as myself. You said it yourself, all beliefs must be respected equally if we are to truly be a free society, especially in America since this is the most pluralistic religious nation in the world.

Mr. COMMON SENSE: I implied that the right of every person to believe as they see fit must be respected and protected equally under the law as well as in social behavior. <u>But that doesn't mean all religions are equal</u>. **No religion is equal to Christianity because there is no equal to Jesus Christ.** One of our great Founding Fathers, Patrick Henry, who fought for adoption of the Bill of Rights had this to say, *"It cannot be emphasized too strongly or too often that this great nation was founded, not by religionists, but by Christians, not by religions, but on the gospel of Jesus Christ! For this very reason peoples of other faiths have been afforded asylum, prosperity, and freedom of worship here."* In his farewell Address, George Washington stated, *"Of all the dispositions and habits which lead to political prosperity, religion and morality are indispensable supports. In vain would that man claim the tribute of patriotism who should labor to subvert these great pillars of human happiness."* Christianity is a religion based on truth and love. Greater love hath no man than He who gives His life for another. For God so loved the world that He gave His only begotten Son, that whosoever believes in Him shall not perish but have everlasting life. Jesus said, "*No man comes to the Father but by Me.*" He will judge us all, no matter what our beliefs may be, because He is who He said He was, the Son of the almighty God, the Creator of heaven, the universe, the earth and everything that lives and creeps upon the earth, including man. We are special because we are created in His image. He will judge us by the amount of love we have for Him, His laws and His creation, including our fellow man. His love is so great He tells us to love even our enemies and overcome evil with good. **Christianity was the dominant belief of the Founders of America and it is the Heritage of this nation that no one has a right to tear down, destroy and wipe from the governmental or public arena.**

Mr. OTHER SIDE: Oh, my poor Mr. Common Sense, don't you see how your attitude could never work in a free society? How could we have peace and freedom with so many different religious beliefs in one nation with one religion claiming to be superior to all the rest? The religious contention would bring us to war-like bickering. How would freedom ever work out?

Mr. COMMON SENSE: It worked out just fine in this country for almost two centuries, until those unqualified Justices of the court erroneously misunderstood the purpose and intent of the Bill of Rights which destroyed our most sacred rights and American heritage. The Founders of this nation understood that freedom could only work if the government respected every citizen's rights to all differences of religious belief by allowing all persons the freedom to believe or not believe as they see fit. They knew that freedom would only prevail when coupled with the maturity of every citizen to be tolerant of our right to have different opinions and beliefs. Every citizen has the right to believe what they will. We have a right to be right. We have a right to be wrong. We have a right to think for ourselves and change our minds if we want. We have a right to exchange differences of opinion and an obligation to respect the right to agree to disagree.

Mr. OTHER SIDE: What a wonderful world of fantasy you live in. My client, the Supreme Court, has done a marvelous job of walking the tightrope between the reality of evolution and the imaginary world of religion. I'm convinced there is no God. There can be no creator when it's obvious we are the result of evolution. Man couldn't be created by some god and be the descendants of apes, too.

Mr. COMMON SENSE: An excellent point, Mr. Other Side. Either evolution is true and creation is false, or creation by a Higher Intelligence is true and evolution is false.

Mr. OTHER SIDE: You're leaving out those who believe in both God and Evolution. So who is to say which is right?

Mr. COMMON SENSE: Don't try to muddy the water. You're speaking of the pitifully confused. They have heard the lie of evolution repeated so often they believe it must be true, but they also believe in God so they assume if evolution took place it must have been God's doing. **The truth is evolution never took place at all, and all things were created by God just as the Bible says.** God gave every man a measure of faith to know God exists, and the fool says in his heart there is no God. To say we are the descendants of apes is not only an enormous insult to all mankind, including yourself, but much worse-- it's an enormous insult to almighty God.

Mr. OTHER SIDE: So now what you're telling me is this "religion of love" has the right to insult me. What kind of respect do you or your god show for my beliefs?

Mr. COMMON SENSE: What God is telling you is that to believe the lie of evolution is an insult to Him. But as far as respecting your belief goes, under the proper attitude of freedom I must respect your right to believe as you want. However, no one is obligated to respect or accept what you believe to the degree of having no choice but to agree with you in order to not offend you. Throughout this proceeding you have relentlessly insulted my beliefs, yet I am not offended by you, even though I disagree with you completely. In fact, I have great compassion on you because you are pitifully deceived. You don't know what you're missing, and you don't know how severe the consequences of your beliefs will be on the day of judgment. There will be much wailing and gnashing of teeth.

Mr. OTHER SIDE: Am I the one on trial here? May I remind you I'm here solely to defend the Supreme Court. Please direct your imputations of guilt to the accused.

Mr. COMMON SENSE: No, you're not on trial. But your lack of belief in God and the actions of the Supreme Court are parallel, because **the Court has unjustly and illegally interfered greatly with our right to the free exercise of religion to the point that it is a severe act of tyranny.** They have assumed authority upon themselves that elevates them to the position of being the dictatorial law-making 'gods' of America determining that whatever personal opinions they have are the "law of the land." They have, and continue to strike down, every vestige of public reference and acknowledgement of God and His laws that were originally respected as the model for the laws of this land and our culture.

Mr. OTHER SIDE: Those references to god must be struck down. It all boils down to whether we are going to respect the fantasies portrayed in the so-called bible, or respect the scientific facts of evolution as the reasonable authority upon which to govern society, because that is the truth of human origin.

Mr. COMMON SENSE: Perhaps you're right about that, except you are deceived as to which is the truth. Earlier I said I would show that it's evolution that is the fantasy, and a creative God is fact. Please allow me to present some compelling evidence, and I will allow you an equal opportunity to present yours. The truth of the matter is that the theory of evolution has been credited to be dreamed up by Charles Darwin, even though some ancient Greeks had similar ideas. While visiting tropical islands, Darwin observed that certain species of birds had similar features, and his imagination went wild fantasizing that perhaps one species evolved from another species by accidental genetic mutations, perhaps over millions of years. As if this macro-evolution theory weren't enough of a stretch of the imagination, he then went on to take a giant leap into the world of fantasy, imagining that perhaps all species evolved from one to another, including the human race which he thought could have evolved from more primitive primates. This would be about as intelligent as aliens from outer space coming to earth today and assuming that since there are similarities in automobiles that Chevrolet's must have evolved from Ford's because they have many similarities such as wheels, windshields and steering wheels. Of course, Darwin's theory was never proven to be fact, and the man even expressed serious doubt in it later in his life after realizing the awesome engineering of the eye was so complicated in design that it could not have evolved by accident. He died a frustrated man because no scientist in the whole world ever discovered even a single fossil revealing an evolutionary transition from one species to another. Darwin's theory is nothing more than imaginary monkey business.

Mr. OTHER SIDE: I resent that remark. Just because Darwin had doubts about his theory late in his life doesn't mean he didn't stumble upon a good idea. Besides, plenty of other scientists have discovered missing links since then, and they have been documented and heralded in a wealth of scientific journals. We have all seen the pictures in textbooks and science magazines showing the progression of evolution from ape to man.

Mr. COMMON SENSE: Please be patient, Mr. Other Side. I haven't finished presenting my evidence of the "lack of evidence" concerning evolution. But to respond to your concern—those so-called missing links the scientific community has so proudly heralded don't add up to anything close to evidence, because not one of those findings can be verified as undisputable proof. The actual finds in most cases were nothing more than small parts of a skull, a jawbone, bone fragments, or in one instance a tooth, that eventually upon thorough examination turned out to be a pig's tooth. The "Piltdown" man and another archaeological find named "Lucy" that were claimed as missing evolutionary links turned out to be complete fabrications by devious scientists eager to fake evidence in a foiled attempt to add credibility to the theory of evolution. Paleontologists may claim to discover a missing link but they have found only a few parts of really who knows what? Then they use their imaginations to fill in the rest and arrange for their guesses to be illustrated by an artist. Those so-called "pictures" you saw in a textbook weren't actual photo's of the progression from ape to man but nothing more than an artist's illustrations. Get real, man! Evolution is nothing more than arrogant fantasy.

Mr. OTHER SIDE: Hah! How dare you demean the integrity of some of the world's most respected scientists!

Mr. COMMON SENSE: In my opinion, Sir, paleontologists can hardly be described as scientists because few of their theoretical conclusions can be verified as fact. Their studies of ancient man and cultures is 95% speculated guesses, often based on nothing more than miniscule evidence, miscalculated personal assumptions and pure imagination.

Mr. OTHER SIDE: Then how do you explain the truth that their calculations are respected as fact by practically all of the scientific community, and educators from kindergarten to the highest levels of colleges and universities?

Mr. COMMON SENSE: It's very simple, Mr. Other Side. Those scientists and educators of whom you speak are too simple-minded to put enough mental effort into the subject to figure out the very simple truths of basic construction and how anything comes into being or is built. But before I explain that further, I would like to point out that a growing number of scientists who have been involved in the advanced scientific studies and technologies of today in the fields of astronomy, DNA technology and the complexities of atoms are concluding evolution not only didn't take place but that it is virtually impossible. Why not follow the example of the most intelligent scientist of all time, Professor Albert Einstein, the great mathematician and physicist who discovered the formula for matter. He wrote about how scientists are possessed by a sense to understand the cause of the existence of all things. Speaking of the curiosity scientists possess, Einstein stated, *"His religious feeling takes the form of a rapturous amazement at the harmony of natural law, which reveals an intelligence of such superiority that, compared with it, all the systematic thinking and acting of human beings is an utterly insignificant reflection."* In other words, Mr. Other Side, the most brilliant scientific mind ever known to man was humbled by the awesome intelligence and precise design of God's Creation. He was the greatest scientist of all time regarding matter and its construction. Do you think you have what it takes to out-think Einstein?

Mr. OTHER SIDE: I am not a scientist. My brilliance in is the field of law, which I would remind you, is the reason I'm here. So I would like to direct the focus of these proceedings to be limited only to matters relating to the accusations you have leveled against the Supreme Court of these United States and not focus upon God, Creation and Evolution.

Mr. COMMON SENSE: I'm afraid you're not brilliant enough to fool me into ignoring something that is at the very heart of the accusation— the people's right to believe as they see fit and to enjoy the free exercise of religion, including public and governmental acknowledgement of God. Obviously, the Supreme Court and many people, such as yourself, have been influenced as to the truth of our existence which directly affects the validity of our beliefs and court decisions regarding freedom of religion. As in any court proceeding, it is imperative to reach conclusions regarding the **truth** of all facts presented. Therefore, I reserve the legal right to pursue the truth regarding creation versus evolution, for we have already acknowledged both cannot be true. I would like to point out that belief in God, or the lack of belief, greatly influences the rulings of all courts and nothing influences that reality more than the false belief in evolution. With all due respect, I will proceed with my objective to prove the falseness of evolution and the truth of creation by God. After which you may present your case for the opposite. Fair enough?

Mr. OTHER SIDE: Fair enough! I will present a very convincing case for evolution and the falseness of belief in God, so feel free to proceed.

Mr. COMMON SENSE: The theory of evolution doesn't make any sense and begins to fall apart completely when thought about in any degree of detail. First, let me briefly outline questions that evolutionists have **never** been able to satisfactorily answer. All of their explanations are **not** backed up with any proven facts or concluding evidence, but are purely theoretical speculation. For instance:

(1) Observe that in all the years since Darwin published his book, "The Origin of Species," outlining his theory of evolution, which was first published in 1859, that not one single fossil has ever been discovered of any living thing from insects to human beings that are in a stage of evolutionary transition from one species to another. **If this really happened slowly over millions of years, there should be billions of fossils to verify every miniscule variance or change. The fossil file should reveal it like watching an animated movie, but there are <u>none</u>!** All the so-called evidence evolutionary scientists put forth is nothing more than weak and pitiful wishful thinking, not conclusive scientific proof of anything.

(2) Evolutionists have never been able to explain, in believable or logical detail, how even a single living cell came into being, let alone give any precise details in the progression of life on earth to the point it exists today. The basic axiom for the construction of anything requires there must be a plan or design, followed by an action to assemble the planned object. Non-living matter has no way to design itself, or assemble itself, no matter how much swamp gas or imaginary bio-soup is applied over any period of time. **If you look at it purely from a scientific aspect, it is mathematically impossible for nothing to accidentally or randomly evolve into something as precise and complicated as the DNA of a single living cell even once, let alone countless numbers of time.**

(3) Evolutionists would have us believe that the elements of life existed in swamp gas or some theoretical bio-soup of non-living matter, and one day a cataclysmic accident or event, such as a great electrical storm, earthquake or meteor collision caused the swamp gas or bio-soup to reconfigure into the precise complexity of a living cell. This would be like laying all of the building materials on a plot of land to construct a house to a certain blueprint and waiting for an accident, storm or explosion to occur to build the house to the exact dimensions and specifications of the blueprint. The random "genetic accidents" that are the heart of the theory of evolution could only destroy, not build or evolve to an improved species. Genetic accidents produce only freaks or death, not a higher form of life.

(4) Some Evolutionists claim that DNA is the intelligence behind the existence of life, but DNA is not a thinking intelligence. It's like the blueprint of a design by a Higher Intelligence. DNA has no way of reaching into the future and realizing all that an organism will need in order to live and survive, including an immune system which it would need from day one, along with the ability to congeal blood and heal a wound. These things all had to be pre-planned by a powerful higher intelligence. Any creature can't wait a million years or even a few weeks for an immune system and healing system to evolve, or wait another million years for a brain and the necessary intricate nervous system to evolve by genetic accident or mutation. And the same is true of all body parts, including the all important heart and complex system of veins, arteries and blood to fuel and nourish the organism, the

respiratory system with delicate lungs to extract oxygen, as well as the digestive system consisting of eyes and ears to find food, a nose to smell it, mouth and tongue to taste it, teeth to chew and throat to swallow it, an esophagus, stomach, acid glands, kidneys, pancreas, liver, and intestines, all to disseminate and absorb nourishing vitamins and minerals, carbohydrates and proteins. Then there's the foundation and mobility system made of bones and limbs, muscles, tendons, and ligaments, all covered with skin, with sweat glands acting as a cooling system; plus there are hormones, pheromones, testosterone, estrogen, hair— and much more. **The simple truth is, no living thing could wait for the complex parts of an organism to develop by the slow process of evolution. All parts would have to be present and in the proper place for any creature to function and live for a single moment.**

(5) Evolution can't explain the complexities of sex and reproduction. If the first of a species were a male, it couldn't wait a million years or more for a female to evolve in order to have offspring! However, creationism does explain it in the first chapter of the Bible, indicating that God created the male and female and every species after its own kind. It is an absolute design of God that he gave every species the ability to reproduce. This 'Reproductive Design' of God is prevalent throughout all of creation, including the seed of plant life. This is another example of the pre-planning that had to take place by a higher intelligence. Do you think it's just a continuous coincidence that every life form throughout all of history always produces generations that are very close to being half male and half female? The fact that the various species of life are made up of males and females, with organs of the right size to fit together for the purpose of reproduction, obviously reveals **life forms had to be pre-designed and engineered by some Higher Intelligence before existence, and couldn't have just accidentally or randomly evolved separately millions of years apart.**

(6) Evolution can't explain how there just happened to be a food supply of plants, fruits and vegetables provided for fleshly creatures to survive, but the second chapter of Genesis does, stating in verse 9, "And out of the ground made the Lord God to grow every tree that is pleasant to the sight, and good for food."

(7) If evolution actually took place and man evolved from apes, why are there still apes, which when they reproduce, results in a baby ape that is exactly the same species as it's parents every time, with not a single trace of any evolutionary changes taking place? If everything evolved, why do all of the old species still exist? Wouldn't those "inferior" species have died out?

(8) If evolution really is the explanation of why life exists, what caused it to stop? There hasn't been any evidence in the entire history of recorded civilization, (which is at least 5,000 years or more) that even the slightest degree of evolution has ever taken place. I would like to state the reason for that. There is no evidence of evolution in all of history because **evolution never ever happened in the first place. <u>It is virtually scientifically impossible!</u>**

Consider this from a purely scientific standpoint. Two competing teams of the most intelligent scientists of our time, using hundreds of the most advanced super computers, raced day and night competing to be the first just to map the human genome. It took them two years to accomplish their goal. DNA is so precise and complex that it couldn't just pop up and design itself and then construct itself. **Using the most advanced technology known to man we don't have the capability to make evolution take place under the most deliberate and controlled conditions in a laboratory. How then, could evolution have ever taken place by pure accident or random chance in the wild over any period of time**? But for the sake of argument, let's assume at some point in the future they do finally develop the intelligence, knowledge, skill and equipment to cause evolution to happen in the laboratory. Then they would have to explain how it could happen on its own in the wild without the precise aid of deliberate intelligence, knowledge, skill and equipment and progressed to the point of life as we know it today.

I could go on with much more that points to the fact that evolution is nothing more than a figment of man's arrogant and prideful imagination, or a desire to NOT believe in God, but just the evidence and reasoning I have presented so far is enough to prove **evolution is fantasy and God is Real.** Mr. Other Side, I'll rest my case on evolution versus Godly creativity if you will just give me an intelligent scientific explanation to any of the questions I've raised, especially my last point-- that if the greatest scientists in the world, using the most advanced scientific equipment, can't make evolution take place deliberately in a laboratory, how could it happen by accident in the wild?

Mr. OTHER SIDE: I uh.. I uh. I don't have to answer the question. I'm not a scientist. I believe we should take the word of those great scientists of the world who have already proved the theory of evolution to be true.

Mr. COMMON SENSE: Wrong! Have you not been paying attention? I've already revealed that evolution is only an unproven theory and the most intelligent scientist of all time, Albert Einstein, believed a Higher Intelligence created all living things and all matter in the entire universe. Now consider this. If man evolved from apes, what caused us to lose so much hair on the body? Which leads us to this question. Why do we wear clothes and feel very uncomfortable being totally naked in public? Animals have no such problem. The answer is NOT something physical that can be explained by science. The reason normal human beings are ashamed to go naked in public is something spiritual that goes all the way back to what happen in the Garden of Eden after man sinned. The Bible tells us before they sinned they were naked and unashamed. Afterward they were ashamed and hid themselves from God, and He made the first clothes for them from animal skins. **We did NOT evolve from lower animals. We are spiritual beings wonderfully created on a higher level in the image of almighty God. Our need to wear clothes is an absolute verification of the biblical account of Creation by God**.

Mr. OTHER SIDE: Big Deal! What about nudist camps? Those people don't have a problem being naked! They love it!

Mr. COMMON SENSE: I said *normal* people are ashamed to appear naked in public. Nudists are getting a thrill out of defying the normalcy of decent modesty. It's similar to the evil spirit existent in the atmosphere of an orgy, only perhaps a little more reserved. And it's not the same as being in public, because all participants have agreed to shirk their normal feelings of shame or embarrassment in a confined restricted area where every participant is guilty of doing the same.

Mr. OTHER SIDE: How ridiculous! It's perfectly normal for sexual partners to be naked and unashamed. What's so weird then about nudists who are just doing everyday activities together in the natural?

Mr. COMMON SENSE: Mr. Other Side, human sexual partners aren't normally naked in public. If you think it's so normal to be naked and unashamed in public, why don't you get totally undressed right here and now and lets see if your face turns red?

Mr. OTHER SIDE: Please, don't interrupt! You said you would allow me to present my case in defense of evolution. I'll thank you to hold your tongue until I am finished. Agreed?

Mr. COMMON SENSE: Agreed. Please proceed.

Mr. OTHER SIDE: Let me point out that it makes a lot more sense to believe in evolution than to believe in an old out-dated black book of fairy tales. I ask our jury of readers to consider this—

(1) Didn't Jesus supposedly say, "He who has seen Me has seen the Father?" Then how could a god whose son was no bigger than a man form all of the matter of the universe, including huge planets and stars that stretch for countless light years?

(2) How could your god scoop up dirt and just breathe life into it? Is that what a man is made from— nothing but dirt? You find it offensive that I say man evolved from apes, but I'm offended that the Bible says we are made from dirt.

(3) Who wrote the Bible? Does anybody really know who composed those bizarre and impossible stories, like a flood that covered the whole earth, with two of every species riding on a primitive handmade wooden boat as big as an ocean liner?

(4) How could a man be swallowed by a whale and survive inside of it for three days, then get barfed up and still live?

(5) Does it make any sense that a man could take the jawbone of a donkey and clobber a thousand men to death with it? That bone would break into a zillion pieces before a thousand blows powerful enough to kill a man could be delivered.

(6) May I suggest another impossibility? What kind of God would turn a woman into a pillar of salt for the simple act of turning around to look at two cities being destroyed?

(7) How could a young boy kill a giant with a single rock from a sling shot?

(8) Here's another preposterous story. Explain how a body of water as wide as the Red Sea could be split apart and the sea floor instantly dried up for a whole nation of Jews to walk across it?

(9) And get this. How can creationism explain dinosaurs? Carbon dating tests indicate they lived millions of years before the recorded history of man. Who created them? You talk of your so-called impossibilities of evolution. What about these impossible things and stories from the Bible? How do you explain these weird tales of fantasy, Mr. Common Sense?

Mr. COMMON SENSE: For a man who claims to be an atheist, you seem to know quite a bit about the Bible, Mr. Other Side. But your ignorance of it exceeds your knowledge. The Bible contains more history and wisdom than any other document on earth. The fact that you don't have the spiritual discernment to understand it doesn't discredit the Bible or God. There are hundreds upon hundreds of prophecies in the Bible, most of which were written hundreds, or even thousands, of years before the prediction took place, and hundreds of them have already been fulfilled to the letter. And not one has been inaccurate or wrong, although some still remain to be fulfilled. That alone should be a spine-tingling revelation of the sacred holiness of the scriptures. By not understanding this, you show very little knowledge of the glorious magnitude of Almighty God. Let me ask you, how much wiser and intelligent is a man than anything he can create, whether it's an oil painting, a sculpture, clothing, a car or a house? Then how much wiser and intelligent must God be than all of His creation? God is so much more awesome than anything our small brains can comprehend that the Bible says the world cannot contain the volumes it would take to tell everything about Him. It also says all things are possible with God. So all of the things you have questioned are possible with an all powerful, all-knowing omnipotent God. But it is impossible to please Him without faith. He who seeks to understand God and comes to Him must believe that He exists and that He rewards those who diligently seek Him to receive his blessings. Faith is the substance of things hoped for, the evidence of things not seen.

Mr. OTHER SIDE: You speak like a child in fantasyland, Mr. Common Sense! Must have faith to believe, hah! That's just some phony scheme pawned off on us by whoever dreamed up the idea of god. I put my faith in the concrete evidence of science as any intellectual person should. I still stand on my belief in the theory of evolution. I say seeing is believing.

Mr. COMMON SENSE: The word of God is foolishness to those who are perishing. That's your problem, Mr. Other Side. You only understand what you can see of this mortal world. You have no understanding of the spiritual world that can't be seen by human eyes. But what have you seen of evolution except an artist's illustrations in a book? To believe in evolution takes a lot more faith than it does to believe in God because, in reality, you have never seen evolution take place with your own eyes, even to the smallest degree, in your entire lifetime. Yet the realities of God's creation are everywhere in nature. You say an intellectual person should believe in science, but apparently what you don't know is that God invented science. He is the truth and factual intelligence behind all of the axioms, maxims, principles and laws of science. Science is nothing more than man's feeble attempts to study and figure out what God has already designed and put together eons ago. Why is it you choose to try to disprove the Bible and God rather than answering the questions I raised about evolution? You didn't counter a single one to prove that evolution took place. Do you believe in evolution because you just can't accept the alternative; the fact that if God created us He might expect some form of accountability, or some responsibility to live up to a higher moral standard than you're willing to accept?

Mr. OTHER SIDE: That's ridiculous! I have very high moral standards, and so does my client the Supreme Court.

Mr. COMMON SENSE: Is that so? Well then, would you kindly explain how being the main accessory to the murder of more than 46 million unborn babies represents a high moral standard?

Mr. OTHER SIDE: Your reasoning is absurd. According to the latest figures available, there's only been around 45million abortions performed to date. The Supreme Court is not an accessory to any crime. First of all, they determine what the law is and what is or is not a crime.

Mr. COMMON SENSE: And that in itself is another crime. The crime of **Tyranny**! Nothing in the Constitution gives the Supreme Court the right, the power, or jurisdiction to "determine what the law is" or to "re-write the laws", or "strike down the laws based on something other than our laws on the books as determined and written by the legislatures. A perfect example of this tyranny is when the Supreme Court struck down the laws against sodomy in the State of Texas based on, of all things, the laws and social standards of FOREIGN COUNTRIES, which is well outside the jurisdiction of the Supreme Court of these United States. I say that's as much an act of treason as it is of tyranny. For your information, Mr. Other Side, in a democratic republic the people's elected representatives of the various legislatures set the rules and write the laws. **The courts are supposed to uphold those laws, not change them, unless they can show where they are in direct conflict with the actual wording and intent of our Constitution.**

Mr. OTHER SIDE: Let's cover one subject at a time. Regarding abortion, the Supreme Court is not committing those acts. They have only given a woman the right to be the sole decision-maker to control her body, not the government. **They have only legalized what used to be a crime in order to give women a free choice.**

Mr. COMMON SENSE: To tell the truth, the Court **has** legalized a crime. The crime of murdering a helpless, innocent unborn child. I'm all for a woman having a choice and being in control of her own body. But when a woman is pregnant with an unwanted child she has already lost control of her body, hasn't she? Abortion is the wrong choice. The time for a woman to make a responsible choice is before conception. Every woman must realize that the female of the species has the unique and sacred ability to start a new life within her body. The fetus is not her body. It's somebody else. Another human being. And the only way to stop that from being another person is an accidental miscarriage or the deliberate murder of the child. That's what the Supreme Court has approved. And **that makes the court more than just an accessory to those murders, they are the main enabling source of those inhumane immoral acts. Especially deplorable are the millions of fully developed ready-to-be-born babies brutally murdered by stabbing a sharp instrument into the baby's skull with the ghastly process of partial birth abortion.**

Mr. OTHER SIDE: Get reasonable, Mr. Common Sense! Most of those unwanted babies are the result of rape cases, incest, or the mother's life or health being in danger. Quite often it's people of poor means who can't afford another child.

Mr. COMMON SENSE: No sensible person is objecting to abortion under the circumstances of rape, incest or danger to the mother, but that is NOT the case in most abortions. Most abortions are the result of an enormously loose moral standard that encourages irresponsible sexual activity, particularly among school age young people, to the degree that **America has become a sex crazy society, entering into it with reckless abandon.** Public school teachers are encouraging young people to have restraint just shy of dogs in heat in the street, then turning to wholesale abortion in alarmingly high numbers to deal with the result. It's an unacceptable solution to morally unacceptable conduct. **To a great degree this is the direct result of the Supreme Court banning God and His moral standards from our public schools.**

Mr. OTHER SIDE: Now who are you to make it your business to determine what degree of intimacy to which people may engage in the privacy of the bedroom? That is no place for the government to stick its legal nose. After all, we all have a right to the pursuit of happiness and privacy. Right?

Mr. COMMON SENSE: I'm afraid the government already has its nose in the bedroom, the back seat of cars, school restrooms, and God knows where else, when school officials indicate, "We know you're gonna get it on kids so just make sure you use one of these" as they hand out condoms, instead of encouraging the safer, more certain, pure and morally decent policy of self-control and abstinence until marriage. Sex was never meant to be just some form of recreational activity. It also has a sacred purpose as God's designed means by which children are born for the continuance of life, building families under the holy and blessed sacrament of marriage.

Mr. OTHER SIDE: Chill out, Dude! That's old-fashioned thinking that went out with high-button shoes. Come on, Mr. Common Sense, get with it! This is the twenty-first century where we're more adult, and we face the truth and reality of life more openly. You're not cool, man. We have to get modern, throw off the old ideas and constantly make changes to improve society so we can be comfortable, laid back and enjoy life.

Mr. COMMON SENSE: What's 'cool' to man may not be so 'hot' with God. His rules of life and righteousness never change, and won't change, just because a segment of humanity gets deceived, goes astray and becomes corrupt. God is the same, yesterday, today and tomorrow. And so are His rules for life. We need to heed the manufacturer's handbook which contains all of the right safeguards of operation and proper use of the product.

Mr. OTHER SIDE: Oh, so now we are reduced to being just a product by your outlandish standards. You are really quite irritating, Mr. Common Sense. And I'm sure those following this proceeding feel the same way. If you have no further accusations against the United States Supreme Court, I am ready to close all discussion, cross examination and questioning, and proceed with our concluding statements to this jury of readers.

Mr. COMMON SENSE: Oh no! There are more accusations of crimes, abuses of power and tyranny of the Supreme Court yet to be presented. But perhaps we should take them up in the next session. Agreed?

Mr. OTHER SIDE: Agreed!

This Session of The People's Literary Court is adjourned until the next Chapter.

Chapter 3

Continued Cross-examination and Closing Arguments

The People's Court is now in order for the Third Session in the trial of <u>The People Vs. Supreme Court Decisions</u>

Mr. OTHERSIDE: What further accusations do you have in regards to my client, the Honorable Judges of the Supreme Court of the United States, Mr. Common Sense?

Mr. COMMON SENSE: Considering the records and some of their decisions, not all Judges of the court could be said to be honorable, Mr. Other Side. It's time to get a little more specific and name names. For example, Justice Hugo Black, a former member of the Ku Klux Klan. Where were the filibustering Democrats when he was nominated? Don't get me wrong. No one should be condemned for their past, <u>as long as they have changed</u>. We all make mistakes in life. And if we learn from our mistakes we will repent and change for the better. That's a matter of maturing. However, as a former member of the Klan, Justice Black apparently never broke the habit of having his decisions influenced by demonic forces. If there ever was someone who was unqualified to sit on the bench of America's highest court it was Hugo Black, who proved he couldn't read the Constitution and understand the purpose and intent of the First Amendment when he wrote the 1962 majority opinion banning prayer in public schools. His glaring stupidity and ignorance of the Constitution, and the integrity of the Founding Fathers who wrote it, is matched only by the other five non-thinking vegetables on the Warren Court who ruled with him at the time. Justice Potter Stewart was the only Judge on the court who had the good sense and integrity to uphold the fundamental Constitutional principle of Freedom of Religion for all Americans.

Mr. OTHER SIDE: **Objection!** Now you've resorted to insults and name-calling in order to prejudice this jury of readers. You ought to be ashamed of yourself for reducing this proceeding to such a low level. Besides, your accusation is outlandish and irrelevant.

Mr. COMMON SENSE: If I was engaging only in insults and name-calling, you may be correct. However, your objection is overruled by the accuracy of truth in my statements that are right on target and very relevant.

Mr. OTHER SIDE: How absurd! You have no right to insult the honorable past judges, or the current judges of the United States Supreme Court. **You can't just accuse a Supreme Court Justice of wrongdoing by uttering demeaning personal contempt.**

Mr. COMMON SENSE: **I have a right and an obligation to tell the truth.** In his decision Black said, "Our history shows that there was a widespread awareness among many Americans of the dangers of a union of Church and State." While it is true, early in the history of the colonies, there was "The Salem Witch Trials," and Massachusetts even banned the celebration of Christmas for a short time long before America became a nation, nevertheless, a concern about the "dangers of a union of Church and State" was never a factor regarding the purpose and intent of the Bill of Rights, primarily composed, or fought for, by Thomas Jefferson, James Madison, Thomas Paine, Samuel Adams and Fisher Ames, and ratified by men of like virtue. **They clearly intended for all Americans to enjoy complete and total freedom of religion, and the free expression of beliefs, with no violation of Religious Freedom by the government.** As Thomas Jefferson said, "*God who gave us life, gave us liberty!*" Jefferson believed that God, not the government, gave us our rights and that the government was not to interfere with those rights. Hugo Black's lack of understanding this basic Constitutional right, and those justices who agreed with the decision and subsequent decisions banning God and any religious reference from public schools and government based on the misconception of separation of church and state, is not only the greatest fallacy of legal judgment in our history, but it has led to the greatest moral decline in America as well. When the court began removing all reference and acknowledgement of God from public schools, in just a few decades, the forefront of American society has become as secular, heathen and evil as Sodom and Gomorra. **The U.S. Supreme Court is GUILTY of being the <u>greatest source</u> of countless crimes and degradation of our culture, depriving several generations of Americans of their right to Freedom of Religion and respect for the high ideals of God.**

Mr. OTHER SIDE: Ha., ha, ha! Don't make me laugh. After that statement, Mr. Common Sense, you need to be referred to as Mr. <u>Non-</u>Sense. They need to have their learning about the phoniness of religion restricted to the confines of churches, synagogues and temples. Or better yet, religion needs to be outlawed completely and branded a threat to our freedom. Bill Maher said on television, "Christians and others who are religious suffer from neurological disorders that stop people from thinking." And he further stated, "We're a nation that is unenlightened because of religion." What's your problem? Don't you see? **The Supreme Court Judges you accuse of interfering with your rights are actually giving us <u>greater</u> freedoms. We need to salute these judges for their insight to throw off the old and welcome many more <u>new freedoms</u> to relieve us from the religious restrictions and inhibitions of the past.**

Mr. COMMON SENSE: Gee, Mr. Other Side, here's another idea you'll probably think is great! Why don't we just make anything and everything legal. That way we won't have any crime. Just let people get as wildly perverted, irresponsible and free as they want. Then we won't need any courts, or law officers, or judges, or corrupt lawyers like you.

Mr. OTHER SIDE: You don't have to resort to being a smart aleck. This is serious. I could charge you with slander (or libel, since this is a book) for such irresponsible demeaning remarks.

Mr. COMMON SENSE: Yes, it is serious when a segment of society is hell bent on pulling away from the decent righteousness of God's laws in favor of a continuously degenerating culture. Since God, and Christianity in particular, have been publicly debased and ruled inappropriate to even be mentioned or acknowledged in our public schools and government properties by decisions of the Supreme Court, this nation has spiraled downward below the gutter. We are now entering into the darkness of the social and moral sewers of America where many people are blinded to the truth.

Mr. OTHER SIDE: Is that all you know is doom and gloom? You are quite boring. Please Mr. Common Sense, make whatever further cynical charges you have against the Supreme Court as the prosecutor's closing argument, and I will follow you with the last word in favor of the defense according to normal court procedure.

Mr. COMMON SENSE: Very well. Ladies and gentlemen, **YOU, the readers of this book, are the jury! You will decide whether the U.S. Supreme Court is guilty or not guilty.** In summary, the first crime I want to impress upon you is that most of the judges, for nearly half a century, and as of the publishing of this book, the majority of judges sitting on today's Supreme Court must be found **GUILTY as charged with bad behavior** in respect to dereliction of duty and incompetence in understanding the purpose and intent of our Constitution, erroneously interpreting the First Amendment to mean, "Separation of Church and State." That is **not what is written**, and that was **never the intent and purpose** of the First Amendment. The Bill of Rights was written to **Let the People be Free**.

The Founding Fathers meant for every American citizen to have freedom of religion, freedom of speech, freedom of the press, and just as important, freedom from government banning of those same basic unalienable God-given human rights. That's what the establishment clause is all about. **It's a restriction on Government**, on Congress to make no laws telling us what we can or cannot believe or say or celebrate about religion. And if Congress is restricted from making laws in that regard, then the courts certainly have no right to make it the law of the land either. **The establishment clause isn't meant to be a restriction on the people, it binds only government, literally walling-in their authority** in order to maintain a hands-off policy regarding the freedom of beliefs, and the free expression of those beliefs for every person, even if they are members of, or employees of the government in the highest or the lowest of positions. The courts have just as much of a responsibility to respect and uphold our rights as Congress does. That's why the First Amendment concludes with the right of the people to peacefully get together and demand correction of what the government does wrong.

And that is what we, the people, must do today. **We must proclaim that the Supreme Court is GUILTY of doing exactly what the first amendment says they have NO right to do,**

namely to take away our unalienable God-given rights as human beings. Misinterpretation of the First Amendment is the main reason America's moral standards have hit the sewer. It's what is behind all of the court cases regarding display of the Ten Commandments, a child's right to pray or read the Bible in school, to have respect for the authority and benevolence of God and ask for His blessings upon ourselves and our nation. It's the major factor causing a movement of persecution toward Christians and destruction of America's Judeo-Christian heritage, the celebration of Christmas and our right to acknowledge God anytime or anywhere, in the pledge of allegiance, on our money, or public displays and buildings. It's what has led to attacks on the Boy Scouts and anyone who upholds the righteousness of Almighty God. This judicial injustice is what has led many people to a lack of respect for our Creator and has proliferated a belief in the falsehood of evolution. No one has a right to separate us from our heritage.

This travesty by the Supreme Court of the United States is an extremely serious offense against the traditional citizenry and history of America over several generations. **Falsely interpreting the First Amendment to mean "Separation of Church and State" is without question a case of Total Incompetence, Reckless Abuse of Power and Outlandish Tyranny on the part of the U.S. Supreme Court!**

In order to make America a free nation once more, you must find these renegade Supreme Court Justices GUILTY as charged with bad behavior because they have stepped far beyond their jurisdiction to assume they are the "Moral Arbiters of America," mistakenly and arrogantly thinking they are the ultimate power in this nation, and that there is no authority above them, including God. Somehow their arrogant ego's apparently blinded them and they have forgotten that America was established as a nation of FREE PEOPLE, a Democratic Republic, where the People are the ultimate power to control our way of life through our elected representation in Congress and the Executive Branch of government. No where does the Constitution give these un-elected judges of the Supreme Court, or any court, the authority to overrule the purpose and intent of the Constitution, the will of the People, as well as the Congressional and the Executive Branches of State and Federal Government. The only way they can properly and legally declare anything unconstitutional is if it actually is in direct legal conflict to the written wording of our Constitution. To take it upon themselves to overrule the actual wording of the Constitution, and dream up warped ideas based on some belief in shadowy meanings "emanations and penumbras" supposedly hidden between the words of the Constitution is an attempt to justify an abstract personal preference that is contrary to the true laws and traditions of American society. **Decisions of these Judges of Bad Behavior, such as the case of Roe vs. Wade, which erroneously made abortion legal, are unconstitutional because there is nothing in the Constitution, no law of Congress, Proclamation of the President, or a vote of the People to make it legal.**

When the majority of Judges on the Supreme Court illicitly made such a decision America was no longer a Democratic Republic but an Oligarchy, which is government with authority vested in just a few. Where is democracy when a handful of appointed officials take it upon themselves to tell everybody else they don't just decide whether an actual law is broken or not, they claim they **are** the law, and whatever they think becomes the law of the land, and the majority of the people have no say in the matter. Let me clarify their jurisdiction and limits of authority. Supreme Court Justices are supposed to determine whether or not the laws have been broken, not to determine what the laws are to be. THEY never were intended to BE the law. The written laws are to be the law. **Justices are simply appointed to America's highest Court to be the administrators of court cases, and are supposed to stay within the confines of judicial procedure regarding the laws on the books and the Constitution, not to break out and rule as kings, queens, gods, or dictators of America.**

This grotesque breach of legal jurisdiction is no more tyrannically displayed than their arrogant and erroneous decision regarding the innocent blood shed by Roe vs. Wade, an abomination of unbelievable proportions affecting the lives of nearly 46 million helpless babies. In various passages, the Bible implies that God knew us, formed us, fashioned us in our mother's womb. Surely God will judge the evil deeds of those Justices who have legalized this atrocity and abort them from a presence in the peaceful and beautiful rewards of Heaven on their day of facing

His judgment. **And you must find them GUILTY as well, to put a stop to this inhumane heartless slaughter**.

Furthermore, you must find the Supreme Court GUILTY in respect to striking down a law in the state of Texas that defined sodomy as a crime, citing laws from Europe as their authority for doing so. Have they forgotten they were appointed to the Supreme Court of the United States of America? What should foreign laws or customs have to do with the laws on the books in this country? Who gave those justices the authority to circumvent our laws and the Constitution? This is another outlandish example of the arrogant pride, ignorance and stupidity some of these judges have displayed in authoring the law by personal opinions, rather than doing what they are supposed to do, which is to adhere to the normal administration of our laws. **You must find them GUILTY of overstepping their jurisdiction and unleashing a perverse evil upon the normal law-abiding citizens of America.**

In addition, the Supreme Court is GUILTY of not understanding the Fifth Amendment to our Constitution. They are very sympathetic toward protecting the rights of criminals by compelling law enforcement officers to read suspected criminals their rights with the Miranda decision, issued back in the sixties, even letting confessed criminals go free if this technicality is not followed to the letter. Where is the sympathy of the Supreme Court for the welfare and common good of the law-abiding citizens of America? Are criminals the only people whose rights matter? The liberal Justices of the Court over the last half century have NOT figured out that the Fifth Amendment was designed by our Founding Fathers for the purpose of **protecting the innocent**, and that it was **never meant to be used as a legal tool for helping guilty people to get out of being prosecuted for their crimes**. It doesn't get much more incompetent than that! That's more bad behavior on the part of certain Supreme Court Justices. Errant decisions of utter incompetence and tyranny by the U.S. Supreme Court have and will continue to destroy the moral fiber of America.

There are many more improper, immoral, and tyrannical rulings that the Supreme Court has handed down in recent times, but any one of the violations I've outlined so far is enough to indict them for bad behavior. The Constitution states they can keep their jobs during good behavior. It's time to ask some judges to leave the bench, resign or be impeached! And who are these Justices? Obviously, the guilty one's of past courts who have set the misguided wrong legal precedents are most guilty, but since they no longer serve on the bench, and most have passed into eternity, it would be pointless and serve no good purpose to indict them posthumously. **We must rid the court of the judges sitting on the current bench today who are GUILTY of Bad Behavior.** As of the publishing of this book they are: Justice Ruth Bader Ginsburg, Stephen G. Breyer, Anthony Kennedy, John Paul Stevens and David H. Souter. All five of these arrogant tyrants of the Supreme Court are tainted with contempt for the Constitution of the United States and the men of high character who originally drafted it, thinking their personal opinions are the rightful constitution by which America should be ruled. They are deceived into thinking they are the law of the land and the people have no power, no authority to be free to decide what we can believe and express publicly in regards to the Christian religion or God. The only beliefs they respect and favor are atheism, agnosticism and secular humanism in the form of New Age thinking and other false doctrines.

They believe they are the masters and we, the people, are the slaves, (the slaves who pay their salaries, by the way). These Justices, that are nothing more than pitiful excuses of judicial fallacy, have been the foils of ruthless, greedy and downright evil organizations such as the American Civil Liberties Union (ACLU). The ACLU is hiding behind a name that is disguised to sound like an upright protector of our freedoms, but the truth is they are a devious anti-American, anti-God, anti-civil liberties organization that has taken advantage of the poor judgment of the Justices of Bad Behavior over the years to spread the social cancer of absolute moral degradation. The ACLU is the legal defense and support for the embodiment of every foul and evil human act and attitude imaginable.

Ladies and gentleman of the jury, what you now decide will have a profound effect on the future of this nation. It will determine whether or not America will return to the respectable position of being a nation under the rule and blessings of God, or continue to float down the sewer of depravity that leads to destruction. We are teetering on the brink of disaster like we have never seen if we do not take up the mantle of God's righteousness

<u>and get America back on track with the same zeal for responsibility and freedom where it started</u>. **You must declare these renegade Judges <u>GUILTY of bad behavior</u> so the removal and/or replacement process can begin. That will allow decent Americans everywhere to have the legal foundation to start a Revolution and Revival of our Rights and freedom of beliefs with the free expression of those beliefs. It will allow us to rebuild this country into the great moral nation it started out to be, a nation we can be proud of once again, based on the high ideals of our Creator, one nation under God, the land of the free, the home of the brave, with liberty and justice for all. Let us have a verdict of GUILTY! Let the Revolution begin! And Let the People be Free!**

The prosecution rests it's case. Now Mr. Other Side, you may proceed with your closing argument for the defense.

Mr. OTHER SIDE: Ladies and Gentlemen of this jury of readers, I beg you NOT to be persuaded by the negative statements of the prosecution. Think positively! **You must find the United States Supreme Court Judges who have erroneously been accused of such serious crimes as incompetence, treason and tyranny to be <u>NOT GUILTY</u>.** They have been great leaders taking American society where it has never gone before, loosening the religious ties that have held us back. <u>We're enjoying more freedoms now than at any time in America's history!</u> Because of the court banning religion, more people can throw off the chains that had us bound for years. Outlawing religious dogma allows us the freedom of living together and having sex before marriage, watching adult movies, all without shame, and being allowed to use more adult language publicly on television and the movies with no shame or guilt about these things that are so harmless and entertain us, while making us more mature, more adult.

It's just the result of the great sexual revolution in America. You remember, don't you? "If it feels good, do it!" What a great philosophy for life! Why have religious restrictions when we can be free? That's what progressive Justices of the Supreme Court did for us when they brought forth the First Amendment principle of Separation of Church and State. It's all about keeping those religious bigots off of our backs and letting us be free to do whatever we like. That's true freedom! Freedom **from** religion. Who needs religion? It's a stumbling block to freedom and that's why we need to keep God out of the schools, out of government, out of the public arena. And hopefully the phoniness of religion will someday be declared a crime in itself and be banned from America altogether, replaced with the scientific truth of elite thinking, intellectuals and scientific minds who know evolution to be the truth.

We don't need our children growing up with phony notions about some imaginary god who supposedly created all things and us. **Let's face it. There is no Santa Claus! There is no Easter Bunny! And there is no god!** Somebody made those things up! The Supreme Court is right to ban acknowledgement of such lies. Mankind is the sovereign ruler of the earth. Why clutter our freedom to be sovereign with the false writings and foolish restrictions of religious nonsense? In addition to finding the Supreme Court NOT GUILTY, we need to thank them for finally, after nearly two hundred years of darkness, introducing the intelligent interpretation of the First Amendment to mean "Separation of Church and State." Thank goodness they finally got it right! They introduced us to the true freedoms we all have desired all along. Shout for joy and be glad we're free. Free at last! Free at Last! Thank them mightily. We're free at last! **NOT GUILTY is the correct verdict regarding Separation of Church and State!**

And because of Roe Vs. Wade, women now have a **choice** regarding pregnancy and their bodies. Thank the Supreme Court for that choice! Disregard that foolishness the prosecution handed you regarding killing of innocent babies. Hey, it's just a fetus, just a glob of flesh. It's not any different than throwing away a piece of leftover steak from off a dinner plate. It's your steak, you can do with it what you want! Right? Of course, I'm right. Any logically intelligent person can see that since Roe vs. Wade nearly 50 million women can't be wrong. And the dedicated doctors and nurses who are making a decent living giving women a choice need to be congratulated, too. **Choices! That's what freedom is all about, and you must find the upstanding Justices who gave us that freedom to be NOT GUILTY of any wrong doing regarding Roe vs. Wade.**

Because of the good judgment of the modern-day Supreme Court, homosexuals and those of various other sexual orientations are making progress toward freedom to proudly and happily practice their lifestyles more openly with equality. Who cares if the majority of Justices based it on laws of Europeans? Let's face it, Europeans are the ancestors of the original authors of our Constitution. Most of them came from the British Isles and Europe. What's wrong with basing a court decision on the laws of people of a foreign country? Supposedly, the writers of the Declaration of Independence and the Constitution of the United States based a lot of their ideas for law on a so-called god. Where's he from? Outer Space no doubt! So whose thinking is more far out? Let's be sensible about this and make the modern, intellectual decision to find our progressive Supreme Court Judges NOT GUILTY of the ridiculous charge of treason for basing their judgment on foreign law to strike down a Texas law, and consequentially all laws of all the States of America, regarding what constitutes an act of sodomy. Don't we have a right to be sexually free?

I can name many more favorable decisions the forward-thinking Justices on the Supreme Court and the various Circuit Courts have made. Thanks to the courts, pitifully incapacitated people like Terri Schiavo can be allowed to be put out of their misery. Think about it. That's a matter of being kind and merciful. Don't we do the same for hopelessly wounded animals?

And what about the Miranda decision and the Fifth Amendment? The Supreme Court ruled to protect the rights of suspected criminals by forcing arresting officers to read them their rights at the time of arrest, letting them go free if lawmen don't. After all, we're innocent until proven guilty. That's a very basic right under the law of the Constitution. List it amongst the things that make this country great.

More recently the honorable judges of the court have ruled to make society better by allowing private entrepreneurs to tear down neighborhoods in order to build projects that will economically benefit the whole community. That's your Supreme Court allowing progress and prosperity. Isn't benefiting the whole of society more important than the rights of any few individuals possession of property?

And in December of 2005 a Federal Judge in Pennsylvania ruled that the farce of "Intelligent Design" is just a disguised version of the "Creationist Theory," which is religion, and has no place in a science classroom, freeing us all from the falseness of God and religion. And I'm certain the elite justices on the Supreme Court will uphold this lower court decision. It's an outrage to accuse such upstanding Justices of truth and integrity of bad behavior.

In January of 2006 the Court upheld a State law in Oregon that allows doctors the freedom to perform assisted suicide for terminally ill patients. **Talk about freedom! I say it again. The Supreme Court Judges accused of interfering with our rights are actually giving us greater freedoms. We need to reward these judges and thank them for their insight to throw off the old and welcome many more new freedoms to relieve us from the religious restrictions and inhibitions of the past. How else are we going to make progress toward a future free of old-fashioned restrictions that make life unnecessarily burdensome and miserable?**

Because of the wisdom of activist judges who have taken it upon themselves to accept the yoke of responsibility to interpret the First Amendment to mean "a guarantee of separation of church and state," such innovative organizations as the ACLU have been able to be pioneers, forging ahead to open up fresh new avenues of freedom from religion for all Americans. We need to thank these judges for their part in making it possible for the ACLU to give America a much needed social makeover. The ACLU is on the cutting edge of legalizing many activities previously thought to be illegal by narrow-minded religionists, thereby overturning old-fashioned, out-dated laws and social attitudes.

In addition to destroying laws regarding abortion and sodomy, the ACLU has supported cases for same-sex marriages, defended open homosexuality in the military services, and legally upheld homosexual education, even in grade schools, to promote tolerance for different lifestyles. Thanks to these judges and the undaunted work of the ACLU, all Americans have a right to desecrate the American flag, to protest the former establishment of society without being punished for this free expression of opinion. The court has often agreed with the ACLU regarding the censorship of displaying the ten commandments and other such religious relics as crosses and nativity scenes. The ACLU needs to be commended for its foresight regarding new freedoms for the future, including support for legalizing harmless recreational drugs such as marijuana, an agenda to legalize prostitution with health inspections to make it safer since we know there are those will do it anyway. We have to be practical and mature enough to accept the real facts of human behavior and adjust our laws to support real life as people want to enjoy it. If people want to look upon naked pictures and engage in so-called pornography the ACLU supports their right to do so. After all, beauty is in the eye of the beholder. Why punish people for having a good time? Therefore, the ACLU takes on cases to support legalized child pornography and nudist camps for teenagers.

And to show you how fair the ACLU is, they even support the extending of legal constitutional protection for terrorists and those who are sworn enemies of America. How's that for loving your enemies? But the ACLU has also proven to be a bulwark against such ancient social attitudes as sobriety checkpoints, drug searches, parental consent laws regarding abortion, illegal wiretapping of citizens, and of course school prayer and use of religious symbols. The ACLU is also opposed to harmful new concepts such as Christian home schooling and medical safety reporting of AIDS cases.

But most important of all, on the horizon is the necessity to enact hate crimes against those who are intolerant opposing homosexuals and various other exciting lifestyles. If Congress won't protect these precious minorities, then it's up to the judges to act on their behalf. **If you find the progressive, innovative Justices of the Supreme Court guilty of bad behavior for striving to give us new freedoms, all of this social engineering and progress will be lost. And wouldn't that be a crime? Let's keep the great ship America on this politically correct course to define new freedoms. Ladies and gentlemen of the jury, you be the judge. It's up to you to determine whether this nation turns back the pages of time to a dull, stodgy society, limiting freedom with unnecessary, irrelevant and phony, out-dated religious rhetoric and ridiculous rules, or whether America will become a truly free society where the rules are few and the revelry is plentiful. The decision is yours. I urge you to cast your jury ballot to keep America on the current newfound**

course of hope given to us by the elite intellectual judges who have pioneered the new freedoms we enjoy today, and bring forth a verdict of NOT GUILTY. America's future is in your hands.

This Literary Trial in the People's Court now retires to the Jury Room of discussion to await a verdict.

Chapter 4

Principles and thoughts for Jury Deliberation

Basic Jury Instructions

In any court trial the jury must reach a verdict based on the truth, the whole truth, and nothing but the truth. The first three chapters of this book serve as a means of cross-examination to bring out the truth by presenting the best arguments for both the prosecution and the defense. Those chapters may be reviewed, serving as a manuscript of the trial proceedings. But obviously, this Literary Trial in the People's Court is different than a normal court trial because there is no judge to give instructions, consult with lawyers, oversee proper court procedure, make a ruling or determine sentencing. And there is no jury of twelve peers to reach a verdict. This literary trial only acts as a venue to expose the truth in an open public forum, and every person who reads this book becomes both a judge and a member of the jury to determine guilt or innocence in their own minds. With such a large number of judges and jurors, not all will unanimously agree on a verdict, and it will be impossible to avoid a split jury. However, a unanimous decision is not the purpose of this trial or this book. A democratic majority will determine the outcome and bring about a demand for a course of action to influence the judicial and moral future of America.

There are two forms of judgment. One is worldly secular judgment with an end and purpose to maintain order by establishing justice or fairness through punishment for those found guilty. Worldly secular judgment often involves blame setting and revenge. The other form of judgment is Godly spiritual judgment with an end and purpose to achieve righteousness and the ultimate good for all concerned. Godly spiritual judgment includes the possible application of forgiveness, mercy and grace above and beyond justice or fairness. Both forms of judgment are often influenced by remorse and the desire to repent and make things right on the part of the guilty. Godly spiritual judgment, which is highly emphasized by the Christian religion and accented by the sacrifice of Jesus, is much more inclined toward encouragement of saving people rather than condemning them, if they have the desire to turn away from evil. This is what is so great about America being founded as a Christian nation. Therefore, if a person is found guilty, and in the process of the trial realized they were deceived regarding their actions, and they regret their wrong choices and want to repent, to change and do right, then the righteous thing to do is to give them the chance to do so. In other words, if any Judge of the Supreme Court who is guilty of bad behavior, yet becomes enlightened to the error of their ways, and expresses publicly a desire to correct all of their opinions of error, as well as past bad decisions of the court, they should be allowed to stay on the bench. However, if they refuse to recognize that their faulty lines of reasoning are truly acts of tyranny, then we have no choice but to begin the process to force them into retirement or impeachment because that Judge is not qualified for the job they hold.

Separation of Church and State

One of the major problems with our modern society is that we have been bombarded with so much false doctrine and downright lies that many people are confused and have no true perspective on what is right or wrong. I would like to state that America, as a democratic republic, did not start out wrong. The Constitution, which was written by men who prayed for God's guidance to help them form the foundations of this nation, and respected the righteousness, power and authority of Almighty God, is not an invalid document, even in these modern times of weakened faith and low moral standards.

The decision of the Supreme Court misinterpreting the First Amendment to mean something that is practically the opposite of how it reads, and does in fact, result in the exact opposite of it's original intent, is both a criminal act of tyranny and incompetence that is a threat to forming a more perfect union, insuring domestic tranquility, providing for the common defense, promoting the general welfare and securing the blessings of liberty to ourselves and our posterity as stated in the preamble of the Constitution of the United States by the Founding Fathers of our nation. This, of course, is the conservative point of view. Now, let's consider the liberal viewpoint of judges on the Supreme Court taking it upon themselves to ignore the actual wording of the Constitution and the intent of the Founding Fathers, deciding their personal opinions as judges are what is constitutional and therefore the law of the land. The modern-day liberal-minded person will assume that's perfectly okay because, to them, the Constitution was written by men with different values, in a different time period, and the Constitution needs to be updated to the people of today, who live much looser lifestyles with less adherence to the strict never-changing moral values of God.

The conservative and liberal ideologies are totally opposite, completely incompatible and absolutely in direct conflict, with no hope of an effective compromise. You <u>cannot</u> retain purity with any amount of poison added to it. Conservative and liberal ideologies are as different as black is to white (colors, not race) and wrong is to right. It truly is a matter of good versus evil. America today is morally split and the only hope of re-uniting is for people to agree on one ideology, or more realistically, for a controlling majority of the democratic republic to agree on the ideology of good. History has proven that if a society becomes totally evil, God will destroy that society as He did with the flood in Noah's time, with Sodom and Gomorra, and various Kings, Queens, governments and entire empires throughout history. The only thing that is keeping God from totally evoking His wrath against today's morally declining America is the body of faithful standing in the gap, repenting for our nation, and calling out to Him daily in prayer.

At this point, those of you who are secular liberal thinkers may find this ridiculous, silly or amusing. If so, you are only proving the Bible to be true. It warns that the word of God is foolishness to those who are perishing. Those who are wise respect the Bible, not only because it states there was a God behind the creation and existence of life, but because of the enormous amount of prophecies given hundreds, even thousands of years in advance, that have already proven to be the true. In addition to being a religious document, the Bible is an historical document filled with hundreds of prophecies regarding the birth, life, teachings, crucifixion and resurrection of Jesus Christ alone, and not one of them was wrong. The odds of that many predictions, that far in advance, being 100% accurate as a matter of random coincidence are mathematically impossible. The life and sacrifice of Jesus Christ is true history. He is who He said He was— the Son of God who takes away the sins of the world, born of God's Chosen People to a virgin Jewish mother named Mary, who was of the lineage of Abraham, a child conceived by the miraculous intervention of the Holy Spirit of God. **The bible is true because God truly exists and is the author of all creation in and of the universe. This is the absolute truth regarding the reality of life, and the existence of all things.** This is attested to by the disciples who saw, touched and talked with the risen Christ. With unshaken faith, they gladly and bravely risked and faced torture and execution, never denying the absolute certain truth of who Christ really was. Those of other beliefs who don't agree do not make the truth an untruth or an uncertainty. They are simply out of touch with reality.

The truth regarding Jesus Christ, God's authority, and creation was the strong belief of the men who founded America. They proved the depth and sincerity of their faith by pledging their lives, fortunes and sacred honor to fight the American Revolution for the principle of all men being created as equal recipients of certain unalienable rights endowed to all mankind by our Creator, and that no man, king or government, has rightful authority to take away or deny those liberties. These unalienable rights were upheld and respected by the people and our government until the mid-twentieth century; when a predominantly incompetent body of Supreme Court Justices decided to break with traditional American and Judeo-Christian values to falsely interpret the First Amendment of the Constitution to mean "Separation of Church and State." And they made this error without even stating a single precedent of court decisions (Stare Decisis). Adding to their legal folly and deception is the fact that, in every court case since the 1962 *Engle vs. Vitale* case, which banned prayer in public schools, the majority decisions of the Supreme Court have falsely been presented as if "Separation of Church and State" was the original intent of the Founding Fathers who wrote the First Amendment. This is a boldface lie and total misconception. Had they checked, they would have discovered all kinds of previous court decisions, precedents that reflected the true intent of the Court and those who wrote the Constitution. For instance, as early as 1799, eight years after enactment of the Bill of Rights, the Supreme Court declared:

"By our form of government, the Christian religion is the established religion; and all sects and denominations of Christians are placed on the same equal footing."

This verifies what has been said throughout *this* book, that the First Amendment thinking from the beginning was, and was always meant to be, that the establishment clause referred only to preventing the government from establishing one Christian denomination over all others as the one and only official religion for the whole nation. The King of England had proclaimed a similar one-denominational ruling, and our Patriots of the American Revolution didn't want that happening over here.

Even though the Framers of the Constitution had strong Christian beliefs they didn't want to make America a monarchy or a theocracy. Therefore, they didn't want to force religious beliefs of any one Christian denomination on all citizens. However, they assumed that basic Judeo-Christian Biblical principles should always be revered and respected in public life, including throughout the chambers of government. If you need more proof that America was established as a Christian nation and our government never was meant to be separated from God, consider some of the words our Founding Fathers espoused. In his "Farewell Address" George Washington said:

"Reason and experience both forbid us to expect that national morality can prevail in exclusion of religious principle. He further stated, *"Of all the dispositions and habits which lead to political prosperity, religion and morality are indispensable supports. In vain would that man claim the tribute of patriotism, who should labor to subvert these great pillars."*

Our second President, John Adams proclaimed,

"The general principles on which the fathers achieved independence were... the general principles of Christianity. Those principles of Christianity are as eternal and immutable as the existence and attributes of God."

If the Supreme Court of 1962 had looked for precedents to support their decision to separate government from religion they would have discovered the original Chief Justice of the U.S. Supreme Court, John Jay, concluded:

"Providence has given to our people the choice of their rulers, and it is the duty, as well as the privilege and interest, of our Christian nation to select and prefer Christians for their rulers."

In 1892 the Supreme Court handed down this ruling:

"No purpose of action against religion can be imputed to any legislation, state or national, because this is a religious people. This is a Christian nation."

Separation of Church and State was the farthest thing from the souls and minds of those employed in America's government and legal system until 1947 when, in the case of *Everson vs. Board of Education,* the court quoted out of context from Thomas Jefferson's letter to the Danbury Baptists and ruled, *"The First Amendment has erected 'a wall of separation between church and state.' That wall must be kept high and impregnable."* They assumed the wall was an **equal separator** from both sides rather than just a restraint on government interference with our freedom of religion. From that flawed reasoning, the Court walked off the cliff of intelligent understanding and plummeted into the pit of complete incompetence and stupid deception with their 1962 decision banning prayer in public schools, which erroneously implied that the Founding Fathers intended the First Amendment to mean any connection between Church and State should be legally taboo. They did this in spite of the fact that in a previous decision one of the dissenting judges on the Court warned that if the court didn't refrain from reference to "separation of church and state" that people were going to start thinking it was part of the Constitution. And thus, the greatest lie and misconception, which is also the greatest blunder in American judicial history concerning the Constitution, was launched. It also led to the greatest moral decline in the nation's history, and continues to deceive most Americans yet today. So, now you know the rest of the story. (My apologies to Paul Harvey for borrowing his signature line).

When Thomas Jefferson penned the phrase regarding "separation" he was indicating to the Danbury Baptists that only the government was walled-in or restricted from establishing or favoring one Christian denomination over another. The truth is—the original intent of the "establishment clause" of the First Amendment was only to prevent the government from interfering with the people's sacred right to freedom of religion. It NEVER was intended to mean "Separation of Church and State." It NEVER was meant to be used to separate God, or those who believe in God, from American government, or to separate children from God in a public schoolhouse. **Without question, the U.S. Supreme Court is GUILTY of total incompetence regarding the purpose and intent of the Constitution of the United States on this matter, and those current judges on the Court who support or agree with this tyrannical error are GUILTY of gross bad behavior. Therefore, we must insist they be removed from the bench.**

Creation Versus Evolution

Evolution is a phony theory because of this factual scientific axiom: Nothing has the ability to design itself and then construct itself. It takes a Higher Intelligence to design and construct any physical object whether still or alive. You may be thinking that an offspring designs and constructs itself. No, that's procreation, the very process of which had to be pre-designed to include the creation of the female. **Nothing randomly evolves into existence**! It is obvious to intelligent thinkers that life and matter requires a complex pre-planning in design and engineering before the precise action to assemble an object occurs. The time is coming when the falseness of the theory of evolution will be revealed with glaring reality. **I challenge those in the scientific community to be humble and honest enough to admit the truth— that evolution has been the greatest misconception in scientific history.**

There are four primary reasons why most scientists have NOT come clean so far. The reasons are: embarrassment, money, deceit and atheism. The most intelligent of today's scientists have already known for years that the theory of evolution is a falsehood that doesn't make sense, but they refrain from admitting it for fear it will be such a great embarrassment to their profession that it would weaken public confidence in the scientific community. In addition, they're concerned too many monetary grants for scientific exploration and experimentation would be lost if they admit the truth. What they aren't considering is, that if they admit the truth about the total phoniness of evolution, many more grants could be attained for exploration and experimentation regarding the truth of creation by a Higher Intelligence. The other basic reason for scientists and scientific organizations endorsing the lie of evolution is that many of them are agnostic or atheistic. They are honestly deceived and full of pride in their own intelligence. Some are totally freaked-out at the reality of the existence of any higher intelligence, other than the scientific society of mankind, especially a powerful entity that might require some form of accountability for the gift of life. There are even scientists who know evolution is false but can't accept the concept of an all-powerful God of creation, so they go to great lengths to dream up some other phony theories such as— "life evolved somewhere in outer space and we are the offspring of alien visitors to earth." They should be intelligent enough to realize that if evolution is impossible on earth, it therefore is just as scientifically impossible anywhere in the universe. An absolute scientific axiom doesn't change with a change of environment. In other words two-plus-two is always four no matter where in the universe we may go. What should we think of someone who calls himself a scientist, yet can't reason any better than that? The Bible says of such people, "Thinking themselves wise they became fools." I call them 'liquid minded scientists.' Because they don't believe in the absolute truths of God, their minds have no solid foundation upon which to intelligently and accurately analyze anything, and their thoughts float around like liquid mercury.

The Godly creation versus random evolution argument was a major part of this trial because belief in God played a major role in the lives of the men who wrote the Constitution and had a great influence on the structure and intent of the document. On the other hand, belief in evolution is the greatest excuse to doubt and *NOT* believe strongly in God. The modern-day liberal Supreme Court has never objected to the teaching of the falsehood of evolution in our public schools, but they condemn the mere mention of the word God, His truths and sacred principles where they are most needed— in a classroom of learning. Learning about the absolute truth and principles of God is essential for a quality education.

Abortion

Before getting into the guilt or innocence of the Judges regarding abortion, I would like to direct some thought to those women whom the Supreme Court has made victims of the *Roe vs. Wade* decision and are suffering from guilt. Remember this— No matter what horrible sin we commit, whether it's abortion, murder, stealing, adultery, sexual perversions or whatever, Jesus Christ still loves us and wants to save us. That's why He endured great pain and suffering to pay the price for our sins on the cross. He did this while we were yet sinners. His forgiveness is a free gift, if we will simply accept Him as our Lord and Savior in prayer, let Him know we are sorry and regret our evil deed, admit it is wrong, express a desire to repent and live by His rules, and ask for His blessed forgiveness. Christ said, "Ask and you shall receive. Seek and you shall find. Knock and it shall be opened unto you." He also tells us to believe we'll receive what we pray for and we shall have it. Do these things and the guilt of your sin will be washed away.

Now let's conduct a little experiment. Find someone who is in favor of abortion and simply ask them this question, "Since you approve of abortion, would it be OK if I pull out a gun and abort you? Or would you prefer that I jab a sharp instrument into your skull, such as a pair of scissor, and suck out your brain with a powerful syringe to abort you?" Chances are they will just stare at you in disbelief that you had the guts to be so bluntly truthful, or they will quickly get the point (no pun intended) and try to ignore you. But if they are outraged enough to say something, most likely it will be a defensive statement such as, "Of course it's not OK. That would be murder!" At that point you should remind them of how completely selfish and totally void of compassion believers in abortion really are. Pro-abortionists think abortion is OK as long as it only aborts someone else's life, not theirs. Are they forgetting that their body too was once just a small fetus in their mother's womb? Would they have approved of it had their mother decided to abort them in the earliest stages of their life? In the absence of abortion the so-called fetus is still a baby human being that will be born and eventually become an adult human being. Abortion is without question the most inhumane cruelty ever approved of by the U.S. Supreme Court. Doesn't the Constitution prohibit cruel and unusual punishment? Abortion is undeserved punishment of the innocent. It doesn't get any more cruel, unusual and grotesquely evil than partial birth abortion in which the doctor jabs a sharp instrument into the skull of a full term baby as the birth begins, and sucks out the child's brain with a syringe. Of course, they excuse this atrocity by claiming the baby's brain is going to be used for stem cell research to possibly save someone's life. What is moral about definitely murdering a new life in order to experiment to maybe someday be able to give someone who is closer to death a chance at growing a new arm or a new spine, when there is no proof a baby's brain tissue is any more effective than adult stem cells or stem cells from blood in the umbilical cord?

So what kind of Supreme Court Justice would plead for criminals to not be subjected to cruelty, yet turn around and call the bloody, heartless slaughter of aborting babies a sacred right? I'll tell you what kind of Judges they are— GUILTY JUDGES! Guilty of approving, aiding and abetting an unusually cruel crime in violation of the Eighth Amendment of the Constitution, the very Constitution they took an oath to uphold when they were sworn in to sit on the bench. The legal Decision of the Supreme Court to declare abortion as a right is a crime of tyranny in every respect of decent conscience. Anyone with any degree of compassionate sensitivity can immediately see the lack of humane understanding in this gross butchery and massacre of the innocent, especially regarding partial birth abortion. It makes one wonder why in the world so many people want to cling to abortion as though it is some sacred, holy right, when the truth is— it is wholly wrong!

Sexual Orientation Issues

This is a very sensitive subject, and again, before we get into the guilt or innocence of the Supreme Court on this issue, I would like to direct some thoughtful consideration toward those who are living a lifestyle of homosexuality or lesbianism. The whole truth is that God is a God of love. The Bible plainly states it in 1 John 4:16— "God is love; and he that dwells in love dwells in God, and God in him." His loving kindness endures forever. It was out of His love that God created all things— the earth, the moon, the stars, the planets and all that is in outer space. He designed and created it because He loved the idea of it. He created everything of and on the earth. He shaped the mountains, the plains, the valleys, the streams, rivers, lakes and oceans. He designed and created all life on the earth from the first blade of grass, the flowers, trees and plant life to aquatic life, the animals, and finally, He created human beings in His own image.

God loved all of His creation and said it is good. But out of all His creation, we humans are the most special, because we were created in the image of God and He gave us a free will. God created us out of love for the purpose of love, and the purpose of loving Him and His goodness. It is our free will that makes us so special to God. Even though God commands that we love Him, He still allows us the freedom to not love Him. If we had no choice but to love Him we would be no more than puppets or robots, with no deep and meaningful worth to our love. But when we do appreciate who God is, respect His authority, understand His glorious ways, love Him and do His will out of our own free will, then our love is immeasurably magnified and made precious to God. It is our free will that makes us valuable in God's eyes when we love Him. His word tells us how to live, and how to love indicating that— if we delight ourselves in the Lord, He will give us the desires of our heart. According to God, love is a matter of giving. Give and it shall be given unto you.

That's why it's so important to concentrate on pleasing your partner in sex. When each partner is focused on pleasing the other partner, they not only enjoy being pleased, but they get magnified pleasure in knowing they have pleased someone else. This explains the principles of God that proclaim— "It is more blessed to give than to receive," and "Give and it shall be given unto you." That is why when we want to please God by being obedient and doing His will that He derives pleasure in giving us the desires of our hearts.

God is a loving creator, and as The Creator, He sets the rules and principles by which all things work for the ultimate and purposeful good. Make no mistake about it. God is the inventor of sex and He has a beautiful and glorious purpose in all that He does. Sometimes we forget he purpose of sex is two fold. First, it's the most intimate physical way for us to express love. Second, sex is the means by which love brings forth the birth of new life to give us children to love. It should be obvious to everyone that sex, as God invented it and intends for it to be exercised, is the union of a male and a female. Physically, the male and female sex organs are designed to fit together to serve God's beautiful and glorious purposes of expressing love and procreation. This brings joy to God and joy to those who do His will regarding sex. The union of male and female is sex. Everything else is sexual perversion. It's why God instituted the sacrament of marriage, to honor and bless the bond between a man and a woman for His holy purposes.

It should also be obvious to everyone that there is no such holy purposes of God in any physical sexual connection between a man and another man, or a woman and another woman. That is the reason why God refers to homosexuality, lesbianism or sex outside of marriage as an abomination. He truly defines it as a sin against His will and His intent for the good of mankind. For those who are guilty of committing sexual sins, I reiterate the importance of asking for God's plan of salvation through the sacrifice of Jesus Christ on the cross. He suffered great humiliation and pain to show us how much He loves us and wants to free us from the bondage and destruction of a sinful life. He paid the price for the sins of all mankind for all time, and whosoever believes in Him shall not perish but have everlasting life. We can be forgiven by simply repenting from evil and believing in the power of His salvation. No matter what you have done wrong, Jesus still loves you and wants to forgive you. Go to Him in prayer and let Him know you want to be obedient to His rules for life, and ask for His forgiveness. It will change your life, and you will feel cleansed and renewed. To those under sexual bondage I say— Don't fall for the Devil's trick of thinking you were born "gay," and that you and everyone else will just have to accept it. Remember this, no matter how entrenched in sin you may be, through belief and faith in Jesus Christ you can be born again and experience a complete spiritual makeover.

When it comes to homosexuality I can speak as an expert on the subject. For over 15 years, I was forced to be close enough to it that I understand how the devil deceives people regarding it. Because of the gay movement coming "Out of the Closet" back in the late 1960's and '70's, I have suffered the loss of two sons. They both were deceived and suckered into the gay community, contacted AIDS, and before they died they witnessed the death of at least 20 of their gay friends, most of whom had also contacted AIDS. My oldest son was the first of my children to die at the age of 32. The coroner ruled it a probable suicide, but I believe it may have been an accident. He had been drinking and went out to a car parked in a closed garage to listen to the radio, because his gay friends didn't want to listen to the music he liked to play on the stereo in the house. The engine was still running when he was found asphyxiated on July 19, 1994.

My youngest son died from AIDS on October 28, 1996. He was 28 years-old and weighed less than a hundred pounds. These were devastating times for me. But God braced me for it 20 years before it happened with a premonition dream. I woke up sobbing my eyes out and my wife asked what was wrong. I told her I dreamed that Mark and Daniel died, one after the other. First Mark, then Daniel. No matter how bad our children can be, we don't stop loving them. You can be hurt and even angered by their actions and bad decisions, but deep in your heart you can never stop loving them. That's the way God is regarding us. That's why Jesus went to the cross to save us from the sins the devil often tempts us to commit.

You may think I'm homophobic or have a vendetta because of these tragedies. Not at all! In fact, I feel sorry for those who are caught up in this sexual perversion trap of the devil. I'm convinced they are deceived and under demonic influence. Before Daniel fell victim to the homo curse, at about the age of fourteen, he asked me one day, "Dad, could we go for a ride?" Once out of the house, he confided to me in the car, "Something has been following me around the house for several weeks. I can see it out of the corner of my eye, and when I turn to look at it, it always disappears. But today, I was in the bathroom and I saw it in the mirror behind me. When I turned to look, it just stared back and grinned at me. It was really ugly and it gave me the creeps." When we went back home we were openly talking about it. My daughter overheard us and said she had seen the same thing. Their descriptions of this hollow-eyed face were identical. Years later, when Daniel was on his deathbed he had come home and I was caring for him. At that time, he told me another story that gave evidence of demonic influence related to homosexuals. One of his gay friends was dying with AIDS and had been in a coma for three days, never moving and very near death. Daniel and some of the guy's other friends had been keeping a vigil in the room during this time. Suddenly, their friend abruptly sat straight up in the bed, opened his eyes, pointed toward the foot of the bed, and with rage screamed, "YOU LIED!" Then he collapsed and died. I asked Daniel who he was pointing to. Daniel said, "No one was there. We were all sitting around the sides of the bed." Then I asked him if he thought his friend might have been talking to the demon that deceived him about homosexuality. Danny said, "Dad, who else could it be? It was scary."

When I got word of the death of my oldest son, Mark, my heart was crushed. But I was determined the devil wasn't going to take him to hell. I had faith that God is still God and is in charge of all things whether any of us are alive or dead. I shouted out with great faith and prayed, "God, you are larger than life or death! Just because someone dies, Oh God, you are still God! You have power over all things and nothing is impossible for you. I know your word says you are a merciful God and a God of love. And that your loving kindness endures forever. Oh God, Jesus didn't suffer and die so He could condemn us, He went to the cross, suffered and died so He could save us." I remembered those passages in the Bible that speak of destruction of the flesh to the saving of the soul. I knew when Mark was a teenager he was mixed up and hating the feelings demonic forces were tempting him to experience. During this time, both the good and bad angels were battling over him, because he went to various churches on his own seeking God and trying to figure out what was happening to him. I knew Mark was confused by the temptations of fleshly lust running contrary to his spiritual desire to do God's will during his life. So when he died I continued to pray, "Please God, take the blinders off Mark's eyes. Give my son a second chance and I know he will choose Jesus."

One night, about a week later, I received another miraculous spiritual experience in the form of a dream that abruptly popped into my head. I saw Mark standing on some form of round platform surrounded by an entire crowd of angels. They did not have wings, but somehow I knew they were angels by the glory of goodness about them. A light began to glow upon Mark's face and he looked upward with tears in his eyes and whispered with heartfelt reverence the name above all names, "Jesus!" I saw Christ in all His glory outstretch His arms toward my son. Mark began to weep and the angels began to cheer with greater zeal than the cheer that goes up when a winning touchdown is scored at a football game. The glow on Mark's face was the glory of Jesus Christ shining upon him. This was a miraculous confirmation to me that God had heard my prayer, honored my faith that He is a miracle worker, that nothing is impossible with God. It was God assuring me that He answered my prayer, gave my son a second chance and Mark chose Jesus and was saved.

I never received that kind of miracle regarding Daniel, but I know he was saved even before he died. In those last months before he passed away he denounced homosexuality and grieved that he had been so deceived. We were very close and I would read him passages from the Bible to comfort him. I remember reading from Revelation 21: "And I John saw the holy city, new Jerusalem, coming down from God out of heaven, prepared as a bride adorned for her husband. And I heard a great voice out of heaven saying, Behold, the tabernacle of God *is* with men, and he will dwell with them, and they shall be his people, and God himself shall be with them, and be their God. And God himself shall wipe away all tears from their eyes; and there shall be no more death, neither shall there be any more pain: for the former things are passed away." When I read that to Daniel it gave him great comfort and he said, "I'm glad you're the kind of Dad you are." Another time when I came down the hall and into his room to bring him food and care for him he told me, "I love you, Dad. When I see your face coming down the hall, it makes my head hurt because I love you so much." I rest assured Daniel was saved. Two days before he died people came from my church and prayed the sinners prayer with him. I pray every day for my deceased sons, and loved ones, because the Bible says to be absent from the body is to be present with the Lord. I ask God to give them a hug for me, show them His love and teach them His ways.

It is NOT a hate-crime to be opposed to homosexuality. It is an act of love to oppose it. Homosexuality, lesbianism and other sexual sins bring death. If it doesn't kill them physically with AIDS, it will surely kill them spirituality with God. If God says it is an abomination, make no mistake about it— <u>it is a sinful abomination</u>! Those poor souls are pitifully deceived lost sinners, and Christians everywhere need to pray that they will see the light and be saved. It's a sin to ignore the plight of homosexuals. We are to be the light of the world and the salt of the earth, not turn our heads away and let them go to hell. Remember, they are deceived. When the gay community wants to declare something in the Bible to be a hate crime, it doesn't take much discernment to figure out who is wrong and who is right. We have a responsibility to stand up for the righteousness of God. We are commissioned by Christ to save the sinners from destruction.

We know who is really behind the push for same-sex marriage and hate-crime legislation. Satan! It's all part of the deception of demonic forces, confusing and deceiving people to take the bait of lustful temptation. Evil spirits are constantly preying upon people whose weakness is seeking immediate gratification in cheap, selfish thrills. The Bible describes today's generation as lovers of pleasure more than lovers of God. That's why drug and alcohol abuse is so prevalent among today's generations of thrill seekers. They are desperately searching for love and don't realize they are engaging primarily in lustful desires of the flesh.. That's why infidelity is also prevalent among homosexuals. Love is a spiritual experience involving the heart, soul, mind and spirit. Lust is primarily a fleshly experience. **Don't be deceived. Homosexuality is not a matter of sexual orientation but a matter of sexual DIS-orientation. It is unnatural love. Not normal!**

For every letter of the alphabet there are words that accurately describe sexual disorientation and same-sex relationships. It is truly—

Abominable, Abnormal, Abusive, Anal, Awful

Bad, Backwards, Bizarre, Base, Beastly

Carnal, Crappy, Corrupt, Crass,

Damned, Deadly, Depraved, Deviant, Diseased, Disoriented

Evil, Erroneous, Extreme

False, Fatal, Filthy, Fickle, Fleshly, Foolish, Forbidden, Foul

Gross, Grotesque, Guilty

Harmful, Heathen, Hellish, Heinous, Hurtful

Immoral, improper, Impure, Irregular, Infected, Inferior

Jaded, Jumbled, Jerky

Kooky, Kinky, a Killer

Lame, Lewd, Lost, Loony, Lousy, Lowly, Lustful

Misdirected, Misguided, Misled, Mixed-up

No-good, Nasty, Nauseating

Obscene, Oddball, Off-beat, Offensive, Outcast

Perverted, Pitiful, Putrid

Queer, Questionable

Radical, Raunchy, Rectal, Reprobate, Repugnant, Rotten

Screwed-up, Shameful, Sick, Sinful, Sodomy, Strange, it Sucks

Terrible, Trashy, Twisted, **U**nnatural, Unsatisfactory, Unrighteous

Victimizing, Vile, Vulgar

Warped, Weird, Wicked, Wrong

X-Rated

Yucky

Zero, Zilch.. It's no where. They need to Zip it and Zap it.

Using the word 'gay' to describe homosexuality is more deception of the devil to indicate the falsehood that this lifestyle needs to be accepted as an equal alternative to heterosexual relationships. It's NOT EQUAL. It's EVIL! Describing sexual disorientation as "gay" is the devil's way of creating the illusion that they are just sweet, kind, perhaps different, yet normal, harmless happy folks. I can tell you from the personal experience of my own sons, knowing and talking to many gay people, and friends of my sons, that they are not happy. Most of them seem to be, and actually are, some of the nicest people I've known, but their so-called gaiety is just a false front for their troubled spirits. It's a cover up, because they know deep in their souls all of the words just listed describes them. They long for acceptance of what they are, but what they are is against the holiness of God because they have been deceived by the enemies of God. The homosexual lifestyle is not an acceptable lifestyle because it doesn't measure up to the standards our Creator intends for the human race. **That's why it is essential for Christians to come out of the closet, set them straight, and save the souls of these poor lost sinners.**

Now let's get back to the Supreme Court's role in all of this mess. For thousands of years, homosexuality was classified as sodomy, named so in relation to the sins of the evil citizens of the ancient cities of Sodom and Gomorrah. The vile men of those communities wanted to conduct homosexual acts with the angels God sent to Lot's house. The people of those cities were so deplorable to God that He destroyed them with a mighty blast of fire and brimstone. The Bible defines homosexuality as an "abomination." At one time every state in the Union had laws against homosexuality, which was classified as sodomy.

So where in the Constitution did the Supreme Court find any legal authority to rule that sodomy was no longer to be regarded in the secular world as a crass, carnal crime against nature, and an abominable sin before God? There was no reference made to the U.S. Constitution, or to any laws on the books anywhere in America that the Supreme Court declared were violated in order to rule that homosexual perversion was suddenly an equal alternative to heterosexual relationships. No, the majority decision of the court was based on their personal opinions which agreed with laws and attitudes of foreign nations. From a legal standpoint, this is an arrogant abuse of power and, as was said previously, tantamount to tyrannical treason.

In order to reach a more intelligent and thorough understanding of guilt or innocence in this case, it is necessary to broaden our scope of knowledge and wisdom regarding the reality of what has actually taken place. The truths revealed by this literary trial are crystal clear and may make one wonder: how in the world could the majority of Supreme Court Justices appointed to serve on the bench for nearly half a century have possibly been so ignorant, stupid or totally incompetent so as to not understand the wording of the Constitution or the intent of those who wrote the document? And even worse, how could they not care, then with pride and arrogance decide their opinions supercede the authority of the Constitution? Another mystery is how the general population could go so long in getting at the truth of this situation, the misconceptions regarding Separation of Church and State, and the phony theory of evolution. How could the court strike down longtime laws on the books against abortion and sexual perversions? **The honest answer is that it fulfills Bible prophecy.**

Jesus Christ told us, especially during the end times, Satan will roam about like a hungry lion seeking who he can devour, that he will, more than ever, exercise his evil nature to kill, steal and destroy. He is the father of deceit and lies, and if it were possible, even the very elect will be deceived. Christ spoke of the time of sorrows and the tribulation which are closing in on us with wars and rumors of wars, nation rising against nation, famines, pestilences and earthquakes. Think about it. Throughout the past century there have been wars and rumors of wars, and modern weapons are more deadly than any in history. In spite of massive charitable relief programs, the world is plagued with death from hunger and famines. Pestilences are everywhere, with new pandemic infections springing up with alarming frequency. Seismologists are recording a continuously increasing number of earthquakes and tsunami's in the world. Hurricanes, tornados, floods, mudslides, huge forest fires and other natural disasters are on the rise. But Christ said this is just the beginning of sorrows. The tribulation is coming! He says it will be the worst of times that have ever been since the beginning of the world, or ever shall be.

Satan and his demons are on a rampage to do the ultimate evil because he knows his time is short. The truth is we're not fighting just against flesh and blood. We're in a spiritual war against the deceit and lies of Satan and his demons. That is why the courts have been messed up for all these latter years. These Justices of the Supreme Court, and many Judges of the Circuit Courts, have been deceived, having the door to iniquity opened by their sins of arrogant pride in the power they have illegally assumed for themselves without authority to do so, aided by ignorance, prejudice and the complacency of people of faith. If you're liberal-minded, you may be irritated or scoffing at this statement, and wondering how Satan and the demons can influence anyone, since you probably doubt the existence of a spiritual realm made up of good and evil beings. If so, again you are proving the Bible to be true, for Christ indicated many would be offended and deceived in the latter times. The truth is, evil spirits look for sinful attitudes in us, our weaknesses they can take advantage of that are in alignment with their evil ways. This is how they hook us. When they come near us they can affect our emotions. Some people even actually become possessed by evil spirits as recorded in the Bible. Once we agree with them they can tempt us, influence our moods and make us feel good about bad things, in which case we will automatically feel uncomfortable with, or feel bad about good things.

Proof of the spiritual world's influence on us is exemplified with the disciple Peter in Matthew, chapter 16. When Christ asked the disciples who they thought He was, Peter answered, "You are the Christ, the Son of the Living God." Jesus indicated to Peter, "Flesh and blood has not revealed this to you, but my Father which is in heaven." Then a few verses later, when Christ announced He was going to suffer many things, be sacrificed and be raised on the third day, Peter rebuked Christ saying, "this shall not be" and Christ said, "Get thee behind me, Satan." Christ was not talking as much to Peter, as He was to the evil spirit that was influencing Peter. Jesus tells us we cannot serve two masters. We will always love one and hate the other. That's why most liberal-minded people seem to be so hard-headed. Their thinking and attitudes are under demonic influence. They are spiritually blinded and deceived because they replace intelligent logical thinking with a "feeling" about people and situations. Thereby, they eliminate such logical thoughts as forgiveness, love, righteous sympathy and understanding and cling to that old "feeling." It's difficult and hurts to see the light when you're in darkness. Many Christians know this and are instructed by Jesus to love their enemies, have compassion for the lost, and pray for them.

So, if some of the Court Judges have been deceived and tricked, is it fair to say they are guilty when we can't prosecute the real masterminds behind their action, namely the demons we can't even see and bring to justice? **Yes, the Justices of the Supreme Court ARE GUILTY and responsible for their actions of bad behavior for the crimes of incompetence, treason, abuse of power and tyranny.** Even though Eve was deceived by Satan, and Adam was tempted by Eve, they both were guilty of disobedience to a Godly commandment. God told them in advance if they partake of the fruit on the tree of knowledge of good and evil they would surely die. In spite of the warning, they ate of the forbidden fruit, and every human being is subject to suffering death as a result ever since. This is very serious. We are all responsible for our criminal actions regardless of who may be an accessory to the crime. Being deceived, even by the demons, is no excuse to escape God's justice.

But there is one exception— Jesus Christ, who is the embodiment of God's righteousness and the expression of His perfect love for us, even when we were yet sinners! By the sacrifice of Christ, we can all be saved IF WE REPENT and turn away from our sins, accepting Christ as our personal Savior. Jesus is who He said He was— the Son of God who takes away the sins of the world. He is a forgiving, merciful and gracious God, and His loving kindness endures forever. **It is the Judeo-Christian foundation of our government that originally brought God's blessings on America and made this country great.** And it is what is left of that heritage that is still preserving us from the wrath of God and total destruction today. Thank God for our Christian heritage.

But because a large segment of Americans have been turning away from God, America is on shaky ground at this time. As a result of the downward moral spiral in this country, God's blessing is not as assured as it once was, and we are seeing evidence of that in the social chaos and tragedies that are prevalent throughout the nation, and the natural disasters that have been plaguing us. The primary source of moral decline in America is the direct result of the Supreme Court's ill-gotten decisions blocking several generations from even a mere acknowledgment of God in the place of public learning. **The Judges of bad behavior on the Supreme Court over recent years are GUILTY of belittling and degrading God, making a mockery of God, and making a mess of our society.** God says He will not be mocked. The day of His judgment is coming. God help those members of the Court when they find out what real judgment is. Let's pray they have the humility to bow down before Him on that day, confess their wrong-doing and repent. It's their only hope, because He is a merciful God. **In the meantime, our only hope of reversing America's moral decline is to clean up the Supreme Court, and get the entire court system back on track showing respect for the high ideals of Almighty God.**

To repeat, Satan and his evil doers are working overtime because they know their time is short. It's the fulfillment of the prophecies of the end times spoken of by Jesus Christ himself. But Satan will not have the last action, or the last word. God's word in Acts chapter 2, verse 17 states, *"And it shall come to pass in the last days, saith God, I will pour out of my Spirit upon all flesh."*

Jesus also said to His followers, *"I will never leave you or forsake you"*.. *"I am with you always, even unto the end of the world"*.. In Matthew 24:13,14 Christ said, *"But he that shall endure to the end, the same shall be saved. And this gospel of the kingdom shall be preached in all the world for a witness unto all nations; and then the end will come."*

If God is going to pour out His spirit in these latter times, and the gospel is going to be taught in every nation, the Lord is not going to allow our rights to honor, worship, pray and ask for His blessing in the public arena in America to be taken away, unless we are complacent, lazy, lukewarm, and too unconcerned to stand up for our rights. **There is nothing sacred, holy, legal, moral, right, wise or good about allowing those who are ignorant, deceived, heathen, lost, wrong and evil to destroy America's heritage as a Judeo-Christian nation.**

So let's be bold, stand up for our unalienable rights and proclaim God before men, calling upon Him in prayer to pour out His spirit and deliver us from the snare of the evil ones just as His word says in the book of Joel, which is reaffirmed in the book of Acts, *"And it shall come to pass, that whosoever shall call on the name of the Lord shall be saved."*

So, where do you stand at this point on the evidence presented in this literary trial? During the trial arguments, if you sided more with Mr. Common Sense, consider yourself to be a person with traditional conservative values who is most likely to be of the Judeo-Christian faith, or at least has a belief in the Biblical account of a God of creation. If you felt more comfortable with the viewpoints of Mr. Other Side, consider yourself to be what is described as a modern-day liberal, who most likely is more inclined to believe in evolution than in a God who created this physical world and life upon it. And if you agree with Mr. Other Side, you can also consider yourself to be among those deceived by Satan. Or perhaps you're in a quandary about it all and don't quite know what to believe is the truth. Regardless of what you believe, always remember, in a free society you have a right to believe it with impunity. In other words, no one should be prosecuted for having an opinion, even a wrong opinion. We should be prosecuted only for evil actions, not beliefs. We should be free to believe, to think and mature and even free to make mistakes in our thinking, but when our thinking turns to actions that are against the laws of God or man we open ourselves to legal, justified prosecution. The belief of every American citizen is important because it determines how we live, our psychological well being, our pursuit of happiness, and most importantly, the eternal destiny of every individual.

What do you believe? Are the majority decisions of the U.S. Supreme Court since 1962 wrong? Are certain judges destroying the moral values of America? Do you believe there are renegade Judges on the Supreme Court, Federal Circuit Courts, State and Local Courts who need to be removed? **Guilty or Not Guilty? You be the judge!**

Chapter 5

Revealing those Deceived by Satan

The Deceived Liberal Judges

This literary document has already established that there have been many judges of the American court system who head the list of those who have been deceived by demonic forces, literally assuming power they were never meant to have, taking illicit dictatorial control over the laws and the Constitution, which influences the lives of every American citizen. But where is the proof of demonic influence, you say? It is revealed by the end results of their actions. The inspired purpose and intent our Founding Fathers insisted upon was clearly laid out in the Bill of Rights, which actually is the first eight Amendments to the Constitution. (The bill of Rights is the first 8 Amendments, although the first ten Amendments were ratified as a package). New York and Virginia refused to ratify the Constitution until it was accompanied by additions that guaranteed the government would never commit the tyrannical acts of violating the very rights the American Revolutionary War was fought to attain. **The greatest of these sacred rights was the right to freedom of religion**, which is why it is the first right mentioned in the First Amendment, along with freedom of speech and freedom of the press, representing protection for the free expression of one's highest ideals.

The Declaration of Independence referred to these liberties as "being endowed by our Creator with certain inalienable rights." Inalienable and unalienable mean the same thing—INSEPARABLE! It means our God-given rights cannot be justifiably separated from us or taken away by the government. So what influenced six judges of the Supreme Court in 1962 to decide they could disregard the wording, and the original intent and purpose of the First Amendment, to misconstrue that we MUST BE SEPARATED from our God-given unalienable rights? Satan always wants to achieve the exact opposite of what is Godly righteousness.

But does that mean the judges who altered the original purpose and intent of the first Amendment to falsely mean separation of Church and State were under demonic influence? Yes it does, especially when you further consider that they always direct separation of Church and State decisions **primarily as an attack on the Christian faith**. They rarely bother to deny prayer, worship or a simple acknowledgement of spirituality to any other religious groups, and they are diligent in defending the rights of atheists in regard to their belief regarding God. The desire of the hearts of these judges of bad behavior gives them away as to whom they serve in the spiritual battle for the souls of humanity. That's why these "Devil Judges" are putty in the hands of the ACLU, which is an anti-American, anti-God group of greedy lawyers who fought to get tax-exempt religious status for Satanists in Rhode Island, while filing papers in New York to deny tax exemptions for traditional Christian Churches.

Another example of Satanic influence upon certain Judges of the Supreme Court is revealed in the fact that they are very sympathetic and creative at inventing rights for criminals while denying rights to law-abiding citizens. They even favor Islamic terrorists— who are sworn deadly enemies of America, Christianity, Israel, Judaism and every other religion and belief in the world. These judges of bad behavior not only revealed where their loyalty is, but they showed their incompetence and lack of operating within the foundation of the law in their decision regarding tribunals for suspected terrorists being held by the military. The five judges on the court who voted to extend Geneva Convention prisoner-of-war rights to terrorist prisoners have failed to understand that the international laws regarding the Geneva Conventions are legal treaties contracted by those nations who signed the legal agreement. No terrorist organizations ever signed or would adhere to the Geneva agreements, and therefore are not subject to the rights therein. Barbaric maiming, cutting off heads, and hiding amongst civilians to make them into human shields and other such despicable tactics as not wearing military uniforms, are not allowed under the Geneva Convention treaties either. But there are those who say it doesn't matter, as a signer of the Geneva Conventions the United States should set the example to live up the Geneva Convention accords regardless. Judges and other liberal-minded mental midgets who follow that kind of thinking are not only stupid, they just have no regard for the integrity of the law. A treaty is a signed contract which legally binds those who sign the agreement, and no signer of the contract is legally or morally obligated to extend the terms of the contract to those who are not only unsigned to the agreement, but are acting in a fashion that is in extreme violation of the contract terms. This is a simple matter of understanding the law. Any Supreme Court Justice who doesn't understand basic law, and can't tell who is part of, and who is not part of, a lawful contract is incompetent to serve in the judiciary.

But incompetent Judges are certainly not limited to the Supreme Court. They are scattered throughout the Federal and State Courts of America. For instance, U.S. District Judge Anna Diggs Taylor in Detroit, an appointee of Bill Clinton, played politics with her court decision in August of 2006 to rule the National Security Agency's warrantless surveillance program to track al Qaida phone calls was unconstitutional. This was just a few weeks after the English, using the same tactics to track al Qaida, broke up a plot to blow up a dozen or so planes that were scheduled to take off from England to the United States. This is outrageous! The wiretapping laws are a joke anyway. I know for a fact that the phone companies can and do constantly tap into phone conversations without a warrant in order to check their phone lines. We need to revamp the wiretap laws to meet the need of protecting America from ruthless enemies who are determined to destroy us in their quest to rule the world. No law-abiding citizen should object to tracking Islamic Fascists who are hell-bent on killing us. Judge Taylor was either ignorant or was putting politics above the public welfare and national security. Either way, she is incompetent to serve as a Federal Judge and should be removed from the bench. And the five Supreme Court Judges of Ginsburg, Breyer, Kennedy, Stephens and Souter, who decided to give terrorists international law protections not only are siding with the forces of Satan, they are a serious threat to the national security of these United States of America as well.

Thank God for the Supreme Court Judges of good behavior who reside on the court as of the publishing of this book, Chief Justice John Roberts, Clarence Thomas, Antonin Scalia and

Samuel Alito. These men deserve our most cherished respect for having to tolerate the burden of being overruled by the evils of those judges of bad behavior who have dominated the court for over half a century. We need to give the judges of good behavior cohorts who will stand with them to uphold the judicial branch of government in an honorable fashion once again. Pray for this!

The Deceived Liberal Press

Certain Supreme Court Justices, and many judges of the lower courts are not the only ones who are guilty of being deceived in these times. Although they have not been directly indicted in this literary trial, it is important to note who else in America the real enemy, Satan, has recruited and tempted into blind deception. Next on the list is the liberal news media that is daily attempting to influence public opinion with demonic propaganda; rhetoric directly aligned with the goals of Satan and in opposition to the will, laws and purposes of God. The liberal news media consists of most large city newspapers such as The New York Times, The Washington Post, The Los Angeles Times, news magazines such as Newsweek, and the radio and TV Network News Departments of ABC, CBS, NBC, CNN and even the BBC. These Reporters are more often guilty of distorting the news rather than reporting the news, because they do NOT go out in search of the truth and report all the facts. They have developed the bad habit of determining what they want the public to believe, and then they go out in search of whatever supports their slanted philosophy. Their news presentation is edited to strongly emphasize their biased prejudices, interlaced with editorial opinion, and is quite often nothing more than evil propaganda. The truths they ignore and edit out of a story are often more significant and important than what is displayed to the public.

Another underhanded tactic employed by these shifty journalists is their misuse of polls to influence public opinion. They first indoctrinate the public with biased reporting, then working hand-in-hand with certain pollsters, conduct polls to see how well their prejudiced propaganda is working on the people. They seldom report or air a view of anyone who disagrees with their intended social agenda (unless it's edited to make them look foolish). For instance, if they interview 10 people and only 3 of the

10 agree with their propaganda prejudices they will edit a presentation showing those three people, and occasionally edit in one of the weakest of those with an opposing viewpoint just to make it look fair. Their goal is to create the illusion in the public's mind that the biased news reports are in agreement with the majority of people in order to create an urge for the public to "get on the bandwagon of popular opinion." They repeat the poll process over and over to create a false sense of the bandwagon growing over a period of time. Quite often they ask a different loaded question of those polled that is never mentioned when reporting the poll results. For instance, they might ask a generic question such as, "Would you rather see America at peace or war?" Then when they report the results of the poll they claim that, "A recent poll shows the vast majority of Americans are against President Bush's decision to go into Iraq." Of course, these phony polls don't necessarily reflect the true opinion of the majority of Americans, and that's why the liberals are often shocked or misread the significance of election results.

It amazes me that these supposedly well-educated, intelligent, eloquent reporters who are trained to dig into hot-spot stories can be so short-sighted and blind to the obvious truth of a situation. For instance, why haven't they picked up on the <u>enormous disasters that President Bush averted for the United States</u> and the world by taking the battle directly to the enemy, pinning them down in Afghanistan and Iraq, and bringing down the tyrannical reigns of the Taliban and Saddam Hussein? Can't they see that Hussein would have been able to easily place significant amounts of biological and chemical weapons in the hands of terrorists by now, and would have been able to eventually deliver nuclear dirty bombs to these maniacs? When President Bush got on Air Force One after being informed of the 911 attack he made an inspired decision to <u>not</u> let the terrorists get by with it like Bill Clinton did when they attacked the World Trade Center in 1993. President Bush made the correct decision to not let terrorists have any privileged sanctuary to train and attack the United States. Thank God we had a president at that time who understood the seriousness of an enemy sworn to destroy the United States and Israel because they are maniacal and deceived into believing their god has appointed this era as their time to take over control of the world. President Bush made the wise decision that any country that co-operated with, was sympathetic to, or harbored terrorists were the enemies of America and the free world. The President sensed the seriousness of the threat and was not going to give this ruthless, sneaky enemy the tactical advantage of being able to attack us offensively at their convenience while we just become sitting ducks for the most underhanded dirty fighters on the planet. It was the right decision to protect our people, our national interests and our allies in the free world. Why hasn't the liberal press picked up on, and reported this truth? They also only briefly covered the story related to the release of a confiscated top secret video of Hussein and his nucleus of honcho's actually discussing Saddam's desire to acquire WMD's for use against the United States.

General Georges Sada was the only Christian in Saddam Hussein's inner circle and was in charge of the Iraqi Air Force. He has defected to the west. In his book, *Saddam's Secrets* he reveals how he persuaded Hussein to change his plans to drop chemical and biological weapons on Israel and the United States. He also exposes that Iraq not only had those weapons of mass destruction, but secretly shipped them to Syria in commercial planes, and in trucks on the ground, when it was obvious the U.S. was going to invade Iraq so they wouldn't fall into the hands of our troops. General Sada and his book have never been mentioned by the liberal news media, and he has only been interviewed a few times on the Fox News Channel. Then in June of 2006 when large amounts of WMD's in the form of Deadly Gas weaponry was reported by two U.S. Senators to have been discovered in Iraq, the liberal press all but totally ignored that news also. These should have been stories the press continuously pounded to death like they did with false reports claiming there were no weapons of mass destruction. But they brushed the truth aside because it didn't fit their propaganda objectives to bash Bush and discredit the Republican Party which greatly influenced the outcome of the mid-term elections of 2006.

Another story the press should have kept as headline news was the attack that ended the life of the evil mastermind behind al Qaida in Iraq, Abu Musab Al Zarqawi. With his death al Qaida in Iraq was weakened, important papers were confiscated that revealed much intelligence and allowed hundreds of successful raids on the insurgent's safe houses. Documents also exposed Zarqawi himself complaining about how effective the Americans have been in overpowering al Qaida in Iraq militarily as well as monetarily, establishing a new Iraqi government and winning the popular support of the Iraqi people. The liberal press still maintained a very negative editorial attitude that dominated their reporting with such comments as, "The document can't be verified as authentic," even though the Iraqi government was adamantly insisting it was written by Zarqawi.

From the intelligence gathered, hundreds of insurgents' hideouts were located, hundreds of terrorists were eliminated or captured, along with large caches of weapons and equipment. This operation was obviously a milestone in the war on terrorism in Iraq, but you would never have known it from reports of the liberal news sources in America. The only hope for victory Zarqawi was banking on was to do what all terrorists always plan to do, simply to win with psychological warfare by deceiving the liberal world press to influence public opinion to favor the terrorists, followed by frightening large numbers of people into submission. The worldwide and American liberal news media agreeing with the cowardly liberal-minded Democrats foolishly play right into the hands of the terrorists' plans, which is to convince enough Americans to cower down to their heinous terrorist attacks to cause us to turn chicken and run. In 2006 that tactic was temporarily headed-off by the Republicans forcing a vote in both houses of Congress to not set a definite date for withdrawal of our troops. How could a so-called experienced former Marine like John Murtha not understand that setting a definite date of withdrawal would put our military, the Iraqi defensive forces, the Iraqi government and the Iraqi people at a very strategic disadvantage and give the enemy the upper hand to plan attacks against our retreating military? We should never announce publicly a deadline date for leaving.

The liberal news reporters understand perfectly well their daily determination of distorting the news to fulfill their goal of discrediting the Bush administration, and they seem to be blind to the whole truth. What they don't realize is we are nearing the end times Christ warned of in Matthew 24:6— "And you shall hear of wars and rumors of wars: see that you be not troubled: for all *these things* must come to pass, but the end is not yet." No matter what political party is in power there will be wars and rumors of wars from now until the time of Armageddon because Christ has warned us so. And fulfilling His prophecy is the fact that Islamic Jihadi terrorists believe this is the time in history when they will take control of the world. This is why Iran's president Mahmoud Ahmadinejad is so hell bent on attaining nuclear capability. He believes he got the green light from Allah to spread Islam worldwide when he addressed the United Nations in 2005. He claims the room filled with a "green light" and everyone was frozen listening to his address. They will stop at nothing now. No sanctions, no negotiations will stop them. Leaving Iraq, cutting and running anytime, anywhere, will not stop them. It will only encourage them. "There will be wars and rumors of wars." Get used to it! These are serious times and reporters are pitifully deceived playing into the hands of relentless Islamic terrorism, and because of their religious ignorance, they are dedicated to deceiving the public as well. Thank God not everyone is falling for it. As Abraham Lincoln said, "You can fool some of the people all of the time, and you can fool all of the people some of the time. But you can't fool all of the people all of the time."

The decline of responsible journalism started years ago when reporters assumed that if something wasn't bad it just wasn't news. They took advantage of the fact that human nature has a bizarre curiosity about things that are tragic, shocking, abnormal, gross or evil. They love to be the bearers of bad news, being in the spotlight with shocking events and alarming situations. The worse the news, the more they love it. That's why they have little or no patriotism. They put their fascination of shocking us with evil above national security and the general welfare of the people. I remember the first airplane hijacking that took place in the late 1950's. The news media was fascinated with this unprecedented circumstance and they just couldn't leave it alone. For weeks every newscast referred to something about the hijacking, even though they really had little or nothing new to report. I remember thinking "What are these idiots doing? Don't they realize they are promoting this, and are going to give other crackpots the idea to hijack more planes?" Sure enough, it wasn't long until someone else hijacked another plane, and it began a string of hijackings that eventually led to the necessity of security check points and inconvenient delays at airports all over the world. The groundwork, in part, for what happened on 9-11was laid by unrestrained sensationalizing of the news regarding the hijacking of planes by overzealous journalists more than forty years earlier.

But what about freedom of the press, you say? **All freedoms come with a need for responsible exercise of that freedom**. We have a license, and are free to drive our cars. But that doesn't mean we are free to recklessly speed, disobey traffic regulations, cause wrecks, and run over pedestrians in order to have something sensational to talk about. There are times when the news media needs to calm down, slow down and steer a straighter, more mature and responsible course.

In the 1970's, two events took place that also influenced news reporters— Watergate and the movie "Network." Watergate gave reporters an intriguing thrill in reporting possible wrongdoing that was highly scandalous at the highest governmental levels. Revealing a cover-up was tantalizing to their zeal to shock and control public opinion. Remember the scene in the film "Network" when a reporter told his TV audience to go to the window and yell, "I'm mad as hell, and I'm not going to take it anymore?" Then they edited to various cuts of people doing just that. This movie gave many news reporters an insight into the promotional power of the press, and they got the idea that they have a responsibility to show no restraints in revealing secret matters (no matter how much it may hurt someone or the nation) because reporters need to use the news media to be the frontline social engineers of society. Even after retiring as an anchor for CBS, Dan Rather said to a meeting of reporters, "We need to make a difference!" No, Dan! Reporters need to <u>report</u> the news and <u>not distort</u> the news, and keep their personal opinions to themselves, unless they announce it's an admission of editorial comment. The news media needs to **report the truth**, and occasionally reporters need to have the wisdom and integrity to exercise the discretion to NOT report even the truth, if it will do more harm than good to individuals, the nation or the world.

The majority of today's liberal-minded news reporters have the misguided opinion that they have "A Right to Know" anything and everything! They think they have a right to pry into, violate the right to privacy, and print anything they can dig up, or come in contact with, even Top Secret classified government information, that if illegally revealed to our enemies would greatly threaten national security. They show no restraint, discretion, integrity or patriotism in the blind quest of their so-called "Right to Know," and to print or report it for the world to see. The news media needs to take an objective look at the destructive and harmful results of their sensationalizing of the news, and clean up their act instead of glorying in it. The news media's "Right to Know" is not nearly as important as it is "To Know What's Right."

Does it ever occur to them that they have the discretion to not print something that is highly harmful? They really don't care. One reason they can't seem to restrain themselves is the pressure of scooping the competition to be the first to report a story, which is a cherished achievement in the journalism profession. The news reporting industry should spend time at some of their seminars to look objectively at ways to restrain from harmful news reporting, but to be perfectly frank, I don't believe they have the maturity or integrity to handle it. More often than not, as time goes on, they can't resist the devil's urge to act like piranha in a feeding frenzy, sensationalizing the news and putting out pure propaganda for political purposes.

What has caused news reporters to become such gossip vultures, seeking out and feeding upon the most rotten material they can consume with a compulsion to vomit it out on the public? The liberal press corps is aligned with the destructive goals of the enemies of God and his followers, and they are GUILTY of ABUSE of Freedom of the Press. A good example of this is their penchant to paint our military casualties as pitiful victims of combat, rather than giving them credit and truly honoring them for their bravery in facing our enemies who cause world chaos and tyranny. The liberal news media, or mainstream news media (whatever you want to call them), are obsessed with reporting a body count of casualties in the War on Terror, playing upon the emotions of non-thinking cowardly chicken-hearted cry-babies like most of the Democrat politicians, who are out to negatively influence public opinion purely for political gain. Nobody likes war, but the Bible indicates there are times when we have to resort to force to combat relentless evil people in the world. God commanded Israel to go out and destroy certain incorrigible evil tribes.

Reporters have acted as though the loss of life or injuries in Iraq was so horrible that Americans, particularly the families of casualties, cannot endure the grief and we must hurry up and retreat from the big bad evil terrorists (who would strip America from our freedoms, our power, and our way of life, if we let them).

And of course, anytime we cut and run that's exactly what the Islamic fascists will do. Cowardice sends a signal to these terrorists that makes them believe that if they persist spreading enough barbarous bloodshed, Americans will all turn like scared rabbits and run. The liberal news media, and Democrats actually gave aid and comfort to our enemies, lowered the morale of our fighting men and women, and prolonged the Iraq war. The liberal news media was an accomplice to the terrorist attacks on American and Allied Forces in Iraq, and elsewhere. Their treason is partly to blame for the resulting casualties in Iraq and Afghanistan that they claimed to be so unbearable.

The unpatriotic, cowardly attitudes of liberals is what is at the very core of extending conflicts. What they don't understand is—terroristic warfare relies heavily on the psychological warfare concept. **Terrorist tactics are to frighten people into submission. Liberal reporters literally play into the hands of the worst enemies to the free world.** To make matters worse, in Iraq and Afghanistan the Islamic fascists have been terrorists conducting covert guerrilla operations against highly visible conventional uniformed forces. Anytime our Allied Forces are employed anywhere in the world they need all the help and encouragement we can give them, and not be additionally terrorized by the propaganda of a leftist press corps. Instead, every single military casualty is spotlighted and headlined by the liberal media with enormous zeal, not because reporters are concerned about the lives of patriotic volunteer American defenders, but because they want to take advantage of the tragedy of war to ballyhoo their liberal agenda to discredit Republicans and the Bush administration in regard to Iraq, while giving the public the false impression the news media is always sensitive and campaigning to end wars and the tragedy of death.

The liberal press and cowards like John Murtha, Ted Kennedy and John Kerry have indicated they are disturbed by the grief of the families of our dead soldiers. If they were truly concerned about the lives of Americans, they wouldn't bother with the small amount of American or Allied Forces casualties in Iraq, which have averaged around 2 or 3 per day. They would concentrate on the huge amount of Americans who are dying in automobile accidents which nationwide average around 117 every day. Do reporters, Murtha and other liberals think the grief of families who lose loved ones in an accident is any less than those who can take pride in the fact that a dead soldier is not just a victim, but a hero? Why don't the liberals campaign against the use of automobiles? After all, vehicle accidents cause 60 times more American tragedies and deaths than any war effort. Or why don't the news reporters spotlight the number of people who die each day from diseases, strokes, old age, domestic violence, drug and alcohol abuse and heart attacks from the stress and depression of watching pessimistic news reports on TV? Deaths related to tobacco and alcohol are estimated in the millions. Once again, the number of tragedies in these areas far exceed military casualties. The reason the news media ignores the total number of American deaths each day, from sources other than military, is that it doesn't fit into their propaganda agenda to influence public opinion for political reasons.

The men and women of our Armed Forces are a bulwark preventing evil worldly forces from taking all of our rights and freedoms away, and we cannot give the brave members of our military enough honor and respect, because we sure don't pay them enough to risk their lives and suffer the hardships of fighting the devils of this world. Say a prayer to protect them. Thank God for those who volunteer to protect us, and honor them with all your heart. The liberal news media needs to realize that if it weren't for the dedicated, brave, volunteer soldiers of today's American military the press would not be free to report any agenda of propaganda. The traitors who report for The New York Times, The Washington Post and the rest of the liberal print news media would like to win a Pulitzer Prize, but the truth is most of them only qualify to be nominated for the Benedict Arnold Award.

More examples of shabby, biased news reporting was done by Dan Rather regarding President Bush's military record, based on deliberately falsified documents. Even worse was the accidental hunting accident regarding Vice President Dick Cheney. The liberal press corps had the audacity to imply that their "Need to Know" was more important than the health and welfare of the victim, all the while recklessly screaming to the public, "Dick Cheney Shot a Man," trying to imply it was a case of attempted murder, when in fact, it was nothing more than an unfortunate accidental hunting incident. Radio talk-show host, Rush Limbaugh, accurately refers to liberal reporters as "The

Drive-By Media," because they take potshots at people with conservative or traditional American values, and delight in their attack like maniacal criminals.

Another series of incidents that influenced the moral decline of the main stream media occurred in the late 1980's with the religious scandals involving Jim Bakker and Jimmy Swaggart. Yes, both Bakker and Swaggart were guilty of hypocritical ungodly conduct without question, and without question it greatly prejudiced the secular press against Christians in general, and their snide biased reporting prejudiced a great many people who were of no faith, or faiths other than Christian. Please note that statistics have shown that the vast majority (over 75%) of news reporters are agnostics or atheists, don't attend religious services, or are inclined to believe that humans exist because we evolved from apes rather than were created by God. Therefore, this group of reporters, to be perfectly frank, are very ignorant of the truth regarding the virtues of Christianity. It also means they are easily swayed to think all TV Evangelists and Christians are hypocrites. Since liberal reporters are ignorant on these matters, they don't realize that it is very errant to judge Jesus Christ by the weaknesses of His followers. Christians may not be perfect, but Jesus Christ is. Even though Christians are encouraged to be Christ-like, God knows the carnal nature of man runs contrary to the spiritual nature of God. Everyone faces temptation, and every now and then we can fall victim to it. That's why God allowed the innocent blood of His only begotten Son, Jesus Christ, to be spilled as the ultimate sacrifice to cover the sins of all mankind and provide a way of repentance for sinners to reconcile their relationship with a pure, holy and righteous God.

An important thing to observe here is the closeness of the occurrence of these two events regarding the Bakker and Swaggart scandals. If you think the timing was just a co-incidence, you need to widen your focus and realize that we are nearing what the Bible describes as "the end times" before the return of Jesus Christ. The close occurrence of these religious scandals fit the plans of the prince of darkness (Satan and the demons), but once again, it fulfills Bible prophecy regarding "the falling away" to occur at the outset of the end times. Baker and Swaggart were hooked by the devil's bait, and the secular liberal-minded press was pleased to expose and sensationalize their sinful folly, also attacking Oral

Roberts and other ministers in the wake of these tragic stories. Because of their ignorance of Christianity, the press, and many non-Christians also, were easily deceived. They need to study and understand the redeeming forgiveness and grace of Jesus Christ. Christ didn't come to earth to condemn mankind. We were already condemned. He came to save us. Repentance from sin is a major purpose of Christianity. The church doesn't claim to be a house full of saints. It comes closer to being a hospital for sinners.

There needs to be a great awakening among today's news reporters to understand where we are on the spiritual clock. Before the appearance of the first man on this earth, a great ageless spiritual war had been raging, and the climax of that war is near enough that it is likely to occur during the lifetime of most people who are now alive. If members of the news media would study the Bible, they would better understand what's happening in the world today, and what's going to happen in the near future. Understanding the Christian Bible and Jewish scriptures is key to understanding the tension in the Middle East, which will be the focal point of a final immensely destructive battle between Satan and his followers and God and His followers. I urge all members of the press corps to be better informed and seek out the truth regarding the Bible, Christianity, and all stories they investigate with the same zeal and open-mindedness as Lee Strobel. Strobel was an agnostic, and a reporter for the Chicago Tribune, who was upset his wife was very involved with her Christian faith. He set out to prove God, Christianity and religion was a falsehood. His extensive investigative research convinced him that God is real, Christ is real, and that it is all real good. He has written at least four books as a result—*The Case for Christ: A Journalist's Personal Investigation of the Evidence for Jesus — The Case for a Creator: A Journalist's Investigates Scientific Evidence that Points Toward God — The Case For Faith*— and— *The Case For Easter.*

The state of today's news media is a reflection of the spiritual war that has been building toward a dramatic conclusion for thousands of years and is no more obvious than the liberal attitude of CNN. In their quest to become the "World's" news channel CNN has become an anti-American, anti-Christian values organization. The Bible warns that being the friend of the "world" is enmity with God. CNN has become friends to the terrorists who provided the network with terrorist-produced video of Jihadist maniacs attacking and killing American and Allied Armed Forces in Iraq. Americans need to boycott CNN and all liberal media sources. Reporters— I urge you to seek the truth! Seeking the truth goes beyond just looking for dramatic footage to support your propaganda agenda, or looking for qualified so-called experts to interview to produce your biased reports. It requires wisdom and discernment on the part of the reporter to know who is credible and who is not, regardless of their reputation. Wisdom and discernment are gifts from God, and if you have doubts about the existence of God, you have no firm foundation upon which to present intelligent and worthwhile journalism. Be well informed with a higher understanding of the age in which we live! Do NOT seek to slant the news to a pre-determined bias, and pass it off on the public as objective reporting. Report the news, and don't distort the news.

I will say this on behalf of journalists— I believe there are many good people who have gotten into the field of journalism, but the very nature of the business is so extremely negative that it opens the door to them being victims of demonic spirits. I believe most of them have been honestly deceived. By that, I mean they are not intentionally vicious but have been led astray by wicked professors of journalism and a constant exposure to evil activity. I have worked closely with reporters in my career in broadcasting over the years. I know one who took a job working in the capacity of a Director for a charity. After many years at his new job, I asked him if he missed reporting. He told me he was glad to get away from it. Until he took his new job, he didn't realize how depressed, stressed and unhappy reporting made him. Just getting away from the evil atmosphere of the worst side of humanity finally brought him a peace of mind and joy he hadn't experienced before. Here again, we need to pray for those in the news media. And we need to praise those on the good side of reporting who work very hard at seeking the truth, fighting the lies and are dedicated to upholding the sound principles of God and traditional American values.

However, until the main stream liberal media reforms, takes a more responsible objective stance, and refrains from reporting propaganda, I would like to suggest that all Americans desert the main stream media and tune to the FOX News Channel, listen to conservative radio talk-shows, read such newspapers as The Wall Street Journal, The New York Post (not the Times), The Washington Times, (not the Post) and go to The Patriot Post, an on-line news service, or check out worldviewweekend.com, as well as Tony Perkins' Washington Update, a service of the Family Research Council. There are many other sources and blogs for getting good responsible news reporting which presents a more middle of the road approach and analyzes both the liberal and conservative points of view.

The Deceived Liberal Political Arena

The contemporary use of the word "Liberal" or "Secular Progressive" that is being used to describe elements of the news media, politics, the courts and social engineering of society is simply a sugar-coated disguised substitute for the words evil, vile, wicked or attitudes otherwise opposed to the righteousness of God. Once analyzed, liberal-secular thinking of these modern times is almost always aligned with Satan and opposed to the will of God. For anyone who is familiar with the word of God, it's easy to spot those who are deceived and campaigning contrary to it.

Make no mistake about it, America today is more divided politically, spiritually and socially than at any time in our history, including the time of the Civil War, a conflict that resulted in more than 600,000 casualties at a time when the population wasn't even 35 million. Even though the political split is more severe today, it is not likely to result in the kind of bloodshed of Civil War times because, for one thing, communications are much faster and ideas are conveyed much more quickly. Today we are more inclined to talk issues out and seek compromises. So at present, our differences have become a war of words rather than armed conflict. That's why it's so important to understand the virtues of the Judeo-Christian faith, which was the idealistic vision for the Founding Fathers of America and is our nearly forgotten national heritage.

Even though propaganda by the liberal press is the greatest offender in causing the largest rift in American social and moral values, they are closely aligned with the liberals of American politics, which is primarily the Democrat Party. I can remember when the Democrat Party was sprinkled with a few statesmen who were patriotic, respected the righteousness of God, and fought for the good of the people and the nation as a whole. When we went to war, both major political parties stood behind the President and our fighting men. They wouldn't think of putting politics above national security by criticizing the war effort publicly, giving aid, comfort and encouragement to our enemies which puts our fighting men and women more at risk. We were a nation united with the determination to win for the good of the country. Today's Democrat Party is a far cry from what it used to be. The lust for power of the Democrat leadership has opened the door wide for definite demonic influence which shows in their political positioning, attitudes and actions. Their primary purpose for existence is simply to oppose everything the Republican Party does, or proposes to do, no matter what dirty underhanded tactics they have to employ to regain or retain dominate power. Democrat politicians will plot, manipulate, lie, cheat, do anything, promise anything, break any promise, and keep a constant smoke screen of propaganda going to deceive the public into thinking they are more moderate than their true liberal intentions in hopes of getting elected. Don't get me wrong, politics is an ugly game, and the Democrat Party doesn't have an exclusive lock on a lack of integrity. The Republicans and other political parties have had their share of politicians who exercised questionable tactics and principles, too.

It's obvious to practically all of us how ugly politics have become by the unethical, mud-slinging ad campaigns they run whenever election times roll around. However, today's Democrat Party by a huge margin is extremely vile, because they have a downright-evil liberal agenda and platform that is driven by their desperate lust for power. If it wasn't for widespread support by the liberal press constantly deceiving people and touting the Party line, the Democrat Party would cease to be a major political force. Please note, I'm speaking of the current Democrat Party leadership, primarily on the Federal level. The real victims of the political battles are the rank and file Democrat voters, people who consider themselves to be permanently Democrats for life, as if a person's political affiliation is as sacred as a religious belief. It isn't! First of all, if the political party adheres to no sacred principles, it's not a sacred thing to claim to be a die-hard loyal member of it. Some say, "Yeah, but I always vote for the man not the party." You can't vote for the man without voting for the party platform the politician is going to be pressured by the party to embrace. If the party platform is foundationally evil, then everyone associated with the party is part of that evil political machine.

The Democrat Party has become an organization with poor principles and integrity. The only principle they respect is getting elected, no matter how low they have to go morally to reach that end. Therefore, they have assembled a coalition of special interest groups they will cater to in order to get votes. Catering to these special interest voting blocks is what they call "politically correct," and it determines what the modern-day Democrat Party platform will be. For instance, they have made the mistake of thinking they can get the vote of women by catering to women's organizations such as the National Organization of Women (NOW). What the Democrat leadership has NOT figured out is—the National Organization of Women no longer represents a majority of women. They only represent the majority of rotten women. How can I say they're rotten? By their demonic attitudes and actions from the start. The National Organization of Women was an outgrowth of the so-called "Feminist Movement" of the last half of the 20th century. The Devil is always deceiving and misleading. Note they called this a feminist movement, when in fact it was an anti-feminist movement. They claimed to be the same as men, equal to men, even claiming they could do all things better than men. All the while, they were rebelling against men. They were in rebellion against God and the Bible, rebelling against marriage, family, babies and everything decent and purposeful about the relationship between men and women. They championed extreme selfishness to be what is best for women. They extolled a career woman as glorious, while portraying housewives and motherhood as the lowest form of female existence. They glorified fornication and adultery, free-sex relations and divorce, while putting down marriage and family life. And their most cherished achievement goal was endorsing abortion in order to eliminate the nuisance of their new-found sexual freedom, namely the birthing of and caring for babies. The National Organization of Women was born out of the pits of hell by demonic forces determined to destroy everything God proclaimed as good according to His purpose and will regarding the male-female relationship. The same demonic forces that deceived women also deceived the Democrat Party leadership into thinking they have the female vote in their hip pocket by supporting the agenda of organizations such as NOW and these evil women's strong call for the false right of abortion. Thank God most women realized Satan's plan for their lives did not make them happy, and they turned back to fulfill the desire for love God puts in a woman's heart to take her place in the family as a wife and mother. Women do have a special role in life, because God gave women the sacred and special ability to be able to birth life. There is nothing sacred about aborting life, something those deceived by Satan don't understand. And there is no greater or more honorable achievement for a woman than motherhood, something we prove every second Sunday in May.

Another voting block the Democrat Party caters to is homosexuals, lesbians and transsexuals. The sexually disoriented want to push so-called Hate-Crime Legislation in order to silence God's righteousness regarding their perversions, and establish legal acceptance of the evil lifestyle Satan has deceived them into thinking is so gay and wonderful and equal to a heterosexual relationship. It is NOT EQUAL! It is EVIL! The campaign for Hate-Crime Legislation is the greatest example of religious intolerance in the world today, and is the greatest threat to the most sacred of human rights.

The Democrat Party leadership will favor whatever agenda this deceived group wants, including selling our rights to freedom of religion, freedom of speech and freedom of the press down the river in order to get votes. Why would the Democrats do such a thing? For the same reason they are in deceived blind collusion with the liberal mainstream news media, as well as those selfish wicked women (NOW), a major segment of the entertainment industry, the public educational system, the deceived liberal clergy, the ACLU and similar anti-God organizations, even the terrorists who are out to destroy America as the world's strongest super power so they can take over the world and usher in the reign of the Anti-Christ. They are all under the same demonic influence! There are those who will read this and proclaim, "Who are you to demonize all of these groups?" **I'm not demonizing them. I am just declaring the truth— and pointing out the fact that they have already demonized themselves which is revealed by their attitudes and actions.** Have you ever noticed how closely aligned these groups are in their philosophies of right and wrong? They are always siding with one another because they have taken a stand opposed to the righteousness of the one true God of creation. Remember, our lives are always a matter of good versus evil. That's the choice we all face throughout life, whether we realize it or not. God said He sets before us good and evil, blessings and curses, life and death, and He urges us to choose the positives.

The Democrats will cuddle up to any group they see as a voting block in order to gain power. The Democrat Party has been able to pull the wool over the eyes of black people more than any other group in America, acting as though the Party of the "Jackass" (the Democrat Party Icon) is the Party that will do the most for this demographic group, while further deceiving the blacks into believing the Republicans are only the rich white people's Party. Have the Democrats ever appointed a black woman to a position as high and important as Condoleezza Rice? The truth is, the only thing the Democrat Party has done regarding black people in recent decades is make fools of them by taking their votes for granted. And now the Democrat politicians are attempting to do the same thing with Hispanics. They see them as the next big voting block they can deceive into thinking the Democrats are the civil rights champions of the Spanish speaking segment of America in order to get their vote. Some Democrat politicians, such as John Kerry, are even learning to do speeches in Spanish for the sole purpose of politically swaying this group. The politics of the Democrat Party are exceedingly vile because they seek to deceive the public in order to get elected, rather than adhering to solid principles, such as the tried and true moral principles of God.

This glaring deceit and lack of principles is no better revealed than by the fact they are even considering deceiving people of faith into thinking they are the party of moral values simply by claiming they believe in Christian morals, sometimes quoting (and often 'misquoting' the Bible) all the while championing the evils of separation of church and state, abortion, sexual disorientation and same-sex marriage. This is not only ruthless hypocrisy; it's a stupid attempt at deception. Don't fall for their tricks to disguise themselves as "moderates" with wholesome family values when campaigning. They will still vote with the rest of their socialistic Party liberals who are more concerned with pleasing "the world" than pleasing God. To show you how ruthless, and lacking of integrity the Democrat Party has become, they are even considering legislation to overturn the laws which prohibit convicted felons from voting because they think most criminals will favor voting for Democrats! That ought to tell you something! And also show the degree of evil demonic influence to which they are willing to succumb. If they thought they could get by with it, their allegiance to evil is becoming so prevalent that it would not surprise me to hear that someday they would try to make a deal with the Mafia in an attempt to swing an election. Or have they already been accused of that in association with Labor Unions? By the way, do you think the disappearance of Jimmy Hoffa was just a mystery, or could there have been something wicked at work there? Of course, the liberal main stream news media would do its best to cover up such a story in respect to the Democrat Party. Why? **They are all deceived and influenced by the same demonic spirits**. Look for the double standards in their rhetoric, the lies and half-truths, trying to hide the truth completely, negative pessimistic attitudes, the two-faced political posturing, always being critical of Republicans while offering few feasible or logical solutions, continuous attempts to deceive, cowardly attitudes and a lack of patriotism, a lack of faith in God, and always calling the righteousness of God something evil. Another red flag revealing deception is the constant proclaiming of the traditional values we were taught to respect as good and right for centuries to suddenly be something bad or wrong, while continually declaring those things God says are evil to be good and "politically correct." The Bible says a double-minded man is unstable in all of his ways. (James 1:8) It was the Democrats who started the lie that President Bush lied us into the war in Iraq, when they knew good and well the intelligence which they all had access to, and by the way, was primarily compiled during the Clinton administration, showed that Saddam Hussein was hiding WMD's and we know for certain he had used deadly gases on the Kurds. His Air Force General Georges Sada reveals it in his book *Saddam's Secrets*. Read it! And we all knew Hussein barred United Nation's inspection teams from Iraq in violation of the peace treaty signed after the Gulf War. If Saddam had nothing to hide, why was he acting like he did? Saddam's lack of compliance alone necessitated going after his evil regime. His pride and arrogance brought him down.

The Deceived Liberal Entertainment Industry

Satan also has the majority of the entertainment industry firmly under his control. This includes Hollywood movie production, mainstream radio broadcasting and TV network programming, the music industry, as well as much of the magazine field and large portions of the book publishing business. We are under a constant avalanche of filth and degradation dumped upon us and our children from these sources. But Hollywood has been the degradation leader for years, driven by their "need for greed," particularly over the past three or four decades. Of course, any business has to make money in order to stay in business, and many movies can be big monetary risks. It's probably easier to lose money on a film than it is to make money, except for the film distributors. They make the easiest, and quite often the biggest, profits of all. In order to play it safe, Hollywood has fallen into a pattern of cultivating a secular audience that will be attracted to theaters by sensationalizing a film with lots of action, which has become extreme violence. Unfortunately, film producers have taken everything to extreme in order to sensationalize, including sexual content, totally trashy and profane language, and depressing demonic storylines. Over the years, film makers have glorified every evil known to mankind, including fornication and adultery, profanity, selfish pride, vanity, idolatry, rebellion, arrogance, senseless violence, greed, foolishness and all manner of worldly attitudes. Too many movies are produced at a comic book mentality level. Their goal is to razzle-dazzle your eyes and ears and freak out your mind with scenes that play heavily upon immature emotions. Once Hollywood produces a box office success they again try to play it safe by making a sequel. That's why there's very little fresh creativity coming out of Tinseltown. They have forgotten that a good movie starts with a good script, and a good script starts with something good, perhaps even virtuous in the story, and is not absolutely dependent on special effects, violence, loose sex and profanity to attract an audience.

However, to be fair and realistic about it, on the positive side there have been some excellent movies produced by this fascinating medium, that if properly used can be educational and inspiring. Most of the great films were produced before the age of the so-called sexual and social revolutions that began in the 1960's, although some good films have been produced in recent years including Steven Speilberg's "Schindler's List," and "Braveheart," "The Patriot," and the "Passion of the Christ" to name a few. The movie industry has been neglecting the original mainstream American audience with their low-class, void-of-decent-content films aimed at a secular male mentality of about 14 years of age. If Hollywood would produce more really good virtuous films, with stories that are truly inspiring and touch a person's heart and soul, they would discover a whole new large market for their wares.

I'm not quite certain why fame and fortune so often leads people in the wrong direction, except that both fame and fortune would likely lead one to think too strongly about worldly things and worldly pleasures, which opens the door for demonic influence. Could that explain why so many Hollywood stars and producers are modern day liberals? Hollywood stars have a tendency to overestimate the political impact of their celebrity. In spite of many celebrity endorsements for John Kerry, and Michael Moore's liberal propaganda attack with the film "Farenheit 911" and 25 million dollars contributed by liberal despot George Soros, President Bush won the election of 2004 anyway. (Too bad some Republicans somewhat ignored their conservative base which contributed to them losing control of congress in 2006). Little impact on election outcomes shows that mainstream Hollywood personalities may have a much higher opinion of themselves than the true mainstream American public embraces. There was a time when the movie industry, and the other entertainment media sources I mentioned previously, were primarily dominated by good attitudes, but then so was the whole of American society. What caused the decline in quality of content from movies, to radio and television programming and the print media? Was it a "Catch 22" situation? Did the public's moral values decrease and cause the entertainment industry to decline? Or was it that Satanic forces influenced key people in the business to gradually loosen restraint, and in order to continuously sensationalize material, sneak more and more lurid, lewd and degrading content into these entertainment sources to make a buck? Could it be the Bible is right when it says the love of money is the root of all evil? Greed opens the door to demonic spirits to control too much about our lives. But thank God, the moral decline of America and the world isn't totally complete, and some decent entertainment is still available from movies, radio, TV and the print media, even if it is available in much smaller proportions than previous years.

The Deceived Liberal Public Education System

The Bible says to raise up a child in the way he should go and when he is old he will not depart from it. That's why the Devil has penetrated the educational system, so our children can be taught lies and to be tolerant of evil, such as the great lie of evolution and the lie that they should learn to be tolerant of sexual perversions, as if it is something good and equal to a normal male-female relationship. And of course, they are being taught that even the word 'God' cannot be uttered in school which gives young children the impression that God is something vile or undesirable. Young people in the public school system today, from pre-school to college, are being hammered into submission to the teachings of demonic doctrine. And what is demonic doctrine? Anything that is contrary to God's doctrine. I urge all parents who care about their children to avoid the public school system, put your kids in private, preferably Christian schools, or home school your children. Most college and university professors are extremely liberal (downright evil) which is a threat to the quality of the so-called higher education. There is no "higher" education than understanding the high calling of Almighty God on our lives. When prayer, the Bible and God were banned from the schools by the actions of incompetent Judges of the United States Supreme Court, the ideal of a quality public education literally went to hell.

The Deceived Special Interest Groups

There are countless special interests groups in America that are totally deceived by demonic forces who are convinced their cause is so politically correct that they are willing to lie, cheat, steal, even kill in order to defend their form of 'righteousness.' Of course, the worst of them have already been mentioned in this document, such as the abortion groups. Groups like Planned Parenthood, for instance. Remember how I cautioned— look for the deceit and double-mindedness of the devil's ways? Just the name Planned Parenthood is deceiving. What they are planning is anything but parenthood, because they are one of the biggest abortion assisters in the world, and are responsible for the deaths of millions of innocent unborn human beings which totally eliminates "parenthood."

Another notorious and deceived special interest group is the environmentalist crowd, such as the Sierra Club. Their wonderful cause is to be fanatically opposed to anything that relates to civilization. Had they been around over two hundred years ago they would have been opposed to Daniel Boone erecting the first log cabin in Kentucky. The wild desire of the Sierra Club and like organizations to keep the earth as wild as possible (excluding big-city night life) has cost the tax-payers billions of dollars wasted on useless environmental impact studies for every construction project that requires clearing any piece of land larger than one square inch in size, since the establishment of the EPA. These impact studies never prove anything, or seldom change anything significantly, and their real purpose is to delay and run up the cost of all physical advancement of civilization from the construction of a simple nursing home, a housing project, a new shopping center, a needed dam or bridge project, every high-rise building and for heaven's sake let's not forget to mention the construction of every Wal-Mart. Catering to environmentalists has prevented drilling new oil wells and the construction of new refineries on U.S. soil for decades, and it has put the United States in the most precarious position of being dependent on foreign oil from nations that are basically our enemies who would like to eventually destroy us.

Some environmentalists are among the most insane-like people on earth. The Earth Liberation Front, (or E.L.F.) who leave their little "ELF" messages after burning down or blowing up new buildings that are under construction, claim their cause to oppose urban sprawl justifies their illegal actions of arson and destruction. This Eco-Terrorism they have engaged in for their "worthy cause" has caused billions of dollars in damages. A related insane organization is the Animal Liberation Front. One of its leaders told CBS's "60 Minutes" from prison that he favors killing a few human beings in order to prevent the death of thousands of animals that are being killed for food. No decent person wants to see an animal suffer, especially at the hands of some sadistic idiot. But Animal Rights groups such as A. L. F. and P.E.T.A. believe animals are the same as human beings and therefore have the same rights as human beings. What is revealing about animal rights groups being deceived by the devil is their misunderstanding about the order and purpose of things as determined by God. God put the animals here to serve man, not the other way around. If members of P.E.T.A. fully understood this, they wouldn't be so psychologically up-ended about the psychological well-being of a chicken that's about to serve the purpose of being part of the human food chain, which is not some kind of atrocity, it's simply well within the order of God's will for mortal mankind to enjoy a tasty meal. Pray for them to understand God's ways.

The Deceived Liberal Clergy

There is nothing so disgusting as to see someone who is supposed to be educated in the ways of God, yet proclaiming to be good and holy for the act of being tolerant of evil. There is nothing holy about tolerating evil, especially the evil of sexual disorientation. When ministers and priests approve of the gay lifestyle, or boast about being gay themselves, it must gag God. It ought to gag us, too. Who do you think Christ was talking about in Matthew 7, verses 20 to 23? "Wherefore by their fruits ye shall know them. Not every one that saith unto me, Lord, Lord, shall enter into the kingdom of heaven; but he that doeth the will of my Father which is in heaven. Many will say to me in that day, Lord, Lord, have we not prophesied in thy name? And in thy name have cast out devils? And in thy name done many wonderful works? And then will I profess to them, I never knew you; depart from me, ye that work iniquity." Who are those who prophesy, cast out devils and do wonderful works? They are members of the clergy. The Bible tells us that, in the latter times before the return of Christ, even the very elect will be deceived. There will be those in the clergy who will be deceived. Look around. Listen to the news. Listen to those ministers and priests boasting about their tolerance of evils of all sorts. They side with the evil liberal news media, agree with and vote for deceived Democrats. They even agree with the evil Supreme Court Justices who falsified the purpose and intent of the First Amendment of the U.S. Constitution to mean separation of Church and State. And, of course, they often agree with the ACLU, the most demonic organization and direct tool of Satan on earth, aside from Islamic fascists.

How can clergymen be in favor of separating God from our government, or separating the government from those who believe in God? Doesn't the Bible say those who build a house NOT upon the foundations of God build it in vain? How can clergymen believe that our unalienable God-given rights to freedom of religion and freedom of speech can be violated and denied? How can clergymen agree with the sexually disoriented for the passage of so-called 'hate-crimes' that literally will declare portions of the holy Bible, that warn us homosexuality is an abominable sin, to be words of hatred never to be uttered in church again? These clergymen are deceived and they are an abomination to God. That's why they should shudder at the thought of Christ saying, "Depart from me you workers of iniquity. I never knew you." But most of them probably won't because they are so thoroughly deceived by Satan. The Bible says woe unto those who enjoy evil and warns in First Timothy 4: 1, "Now the Spirit speaks expressly, that in the latter times some shall depart from the faith, giving heed to seducing spirits, and doctrines of devils." In Second Timothy 4: 3-4 (NIV) the Apostle Paul warns, "For the time will come when men will not put up with sound doctrine, instead, to suit their own desires, they will gather around them a great number of teachers to say what their itching ears want to hear. They will turn away from the truth and turn aside to myths." The King James version phrases it this way, "For the time will come when they will not endure sound doctrine; but after their own lusts shall they heap to themselves teachers, having itching ears; And they shall turn away their ears from the truth, and shall be turned unto fables." How accurately this relates to the attitudes of the sexually disoriented today? The deceived clergy teaches tolerance of an abominable lustful evil and provides them with the acceptance their ears are itching to hear so they can feel justified in their fleshly lusts. From another perspective, could one of the myths or fables Paul refers to in this scripture be the lie of evolution, and God's creation the truthful sound doctrine from which men of these latter times are turning away? Some members of the deceived liberal clergy have been duped into believing God created by the process of evolution. It's hard to believe intelligent people and learned Biblical scholars can be so unwise.

The most deceived clergy in the entire world are the Islamic Jihadist Neo-Nazi Fascists who are deceived into thinking they are worshiping God. Where do their intense hatred and murderous attitudes originate? Why is their hatred directed toward God's chosen people and Christians? Why are they so intent on destroying these members of their fellow man more than any other religions, which they also call infidels, with a warped hatred so intense as to desire suicide to accomplish their mission? The answer is they are hopelessly and pitifully deceived. At least the Satanists know they are worshipping the Prince of Darkness.

We are living in what the Bible describes as the "latter times." All of the afore mentioned groups are deceived and spreading much deception, calling good evil and evil good, and causing great confusion amongst those who do not have a strong foundation in God. Obedient Christians need to pray for all of these lost groups of people who are deceived by the Prince of Lies, the great deceiver, Satan himself and his spiritual clan who rule over the kingdom of darkness. Satan and those who follow his evil ways are already defeated foes by the righteousness of God and the sacrifice of Jesus Christ. Pray for those who are deceived in this life on earth to be freed from the clutches of wickedness. You may be asking yourself why I mentioned all of these deceived groups in this book dealing primarily with the Supreme Court. The reason is **they are naïve, deceived, and on the enemy's team!** They are the people who will rise up to oppose this movement which upholds the righteousness of truth and God's plans for humanity. Almost all of these liberal groups are so deceived that they have no clue they are like-minded, and unwittingly playing into the hands of the most evil powers in the universe.

Some people may wonder if God really exists why doesn't He do something about evil things? The answer is— He is doing something. He's observing all of us. God is perfectly in control no matter how out-of-control fallen angels and mere mortals may become. He is giving us all a chance to reveal our true colors, our true nature, not only for Him to see, but for us to see our true selves as well, so we will have no one to blame but ourselves on our judgment day. Revelation 21 reveals that God created all things for Himself. He created us in His image out of love, for the purpose of love— the purpose of loving Him and His glorious righteousness. As was stated earlier in this book, God gave us a free will in order to make our choice to love Him an immeasurably valuable treasure. This life we now live is a test to see how much we love Him by being obedient to His will and His glorious desire for a beautiful and perfect life for eternity. Life is not about our will. It's all about His will. God is eternal. He thinks in eternal terms. His judgment is eternal. His blessing is eternal. That's why God has a different perspective of the little time we spend in this world. He is more concerned about our eternal life. The Lord will sort us out like farmers of old sorted the wheat from the chaff. The good will be saved and the bad will be cast into the fire. God has His own time table to sort out who will live in perfect harmony with Him in a Heavenly realm. The Bible tells us God is constantly searching the hearts of humanity looking at the good and the evil. I ask you to search your own heart. Who's side are you on? The fallen one Satan? Or the Almighty God of all creation? Who will stand up for God's righteousness, for that which is truly right and not give an inch to the devils who are wrong? It's Satan who is in trouble, and trouble loves company. When you face eternity, will you be keeping the devils company, or will you be in the company of God's people? The answer will determine your fate forever.

Chapter 6

Starting the Revolution for the Revival of Our Rights

What can we do to combat Satan's clan and those lies and tricks devils use to deceive people? If we turn to God for the answer and pray for our leaders, both Democrats and Republicans, to respect the requests of the people to reclaim our God-given unalienable rights: if enough Values Voters can spread the word quickly enough on the internet to start an American Revolution by an organization known as The New Patriots of America (details in Chapter 7) here's a vision of what the future may hold in the last half of 2008:

Imagine the pandemonium as President Bush calls a news conference to announce he's eliminating the jobs of two Judges on the U. S. Supreme Court, Ruth Bader Ginsburg and Stephen G. Breyer. And a newly formed group of dedicated American Citizens calling themselves the New Patriots of America announce, "The Revolution has begun! The Revolution for the Revival of our unalienable God-given rights to Freedom of Religion, Freedom of Speech, Freedom of the Press and Freedom from government tyranny prohibiting these rights is well underway. This is a great victory in the war to turn the tide of moral corruption in this country."

The liberal press, and the liberal Democrats especially, would roar into panic mode as they realize, that if President Bush is successful in eliminating two job positions for judges, the Supreme Court would go from a <u>liberal majority</u> of 5 to 4 to a <u>conservative majority</u> of 4 to 3 creating the first conservative Supreme Court in well over a half century. At the news conference picture ABC's White House correspondent Terry Moran, asking the President, "Sir, would you explain to the American people what gives you the authority to take this unprecedented action? And, if it's just your personal opinion, wouldn't that be abuse of power on your part?" To which President Bush would probably answer, "Absolutely not! Article II, Section 3 of the Constitution says, 'The President shall take care that the laws be faithfully executed.' The problem with the laws being faithfully executed in America for the last five decades is not abuse of power by the President! It's abuse of power by tyrannical Supreme Court Justices who assumed authority they had no legal grounds to possess. When they claim the true Constitution of the United States, which is the legal foundation of our country that they take an oath to uphold, is no longer a valid document, and further claim their opinions form some kind of new murky-gray, 'liquid' or 'living' constitution based on their personal opinions, they are the ones who are guilty of abuse of power. And when Supreme Court Justices go outside the law and the authority of the Constitution to assume power upon themselves making them judicial dictators of America that's outrageous tyranny. What do we call people who go outside the law? Where I come from we call them outlaws, and we don't need outlaws corrupting the judicial system of America. It's the job of the President to see to it the laws are faithfully executed. I'm just facing up to my responsibility as President of the United States to clean up the court system from the top down. "

Moran might do a quick follow-up, "With all due respect Mr. Bush, haven't you been guilty of going outside the law to wire-tap phones of American citizens? And even a member of your own Party, Arlen Specter, has criticized you for taking 'signing statements' on congressional bills far beyond the custom. Where do you get authority for these actions?"

The President might say, "That's not the subject of this news conference. But to answer your question— I haven't gone outside the law at all. I'm attending to my duty to protect the people and our country. The Constitution says the President is the Commander in Chief of the Armed Forces and I swore an oath to preserve, protect and defend the Constitution of the United States to the best of my ability, and one of the main purposes the Constitution requires of the President, and the government as a whole, is to provide for the common defense of the nation. No laws have been broken, but many terrorist plots and cells were broken up. And a lot of these Jihadi terrorists who are out to destroy America, because they think God has ordained that's it's their time to take over the world, were tracked down, and wiped out, like the barbaric madman Al Zarqawi. Defense is the main responsibility the Commander in Chief has. Now uh.. what was the other thing?.. Oh yeah! As far as signing statements go— it's not against the law for the President to express his opinion when signing a bill. That's been a long time tradition for Presidents of both parties. Next question. I uh, I see Helen Thomas is chomping at the bit."

In case you're not familiar with her, Helen is the surly pit-bull-sweetheart of the "liberal blue-bloods" who has attended just about every Presidential news conference since probably about the time of Abraham Lincoln. At least, we can assume she would have loved to have been there so she could have agitated the first Republican President. She is currently a news correspondent for the Hearst News Service and has been known to say she wakes up each morning asking herself, "Who can I hate today?" She would probably respond to the President this way—

"Thank you, Mr. President. I'm NOT chomping at the bit. I'm chomping at the 'Bush.' Why attack the jobs of Ginsburg and Breyer? Don't you realize that most people are going to see this action of eliminating the only woman on the court as being very sexist? And on the basis of fairness, wouldn't it make more sense to dump the judges with the least seniority, Roberts and Alito? But most importantly, how can you claim you're not guilty of abuse of power, and violating the separation of powers, by literally firing judges that are Constitutionally appointed for life?"

Can't you see President Bush looking slightly bewildered before gently smiling to say—

"Well, uh.. first of all, is that a question or an editorial? Now, let me explain— I'm not firing anybody. I'm just cutting back on the number of judges on the court. I'm asking them to retire with their due benefits. Ruth Bader Ginsburg topped the list because she has been going around bragging for years about being an author of the so-called 'liquid or living constitution' which is based only upon the opinions of court judges and, I would like to point out, purely as a matter of law, no liquid or living constitution shows up as a legitimate legal document in the congressional record. The real Constitution, which was signed by the Founding Fathers of America with final State ratification in 1791, is the true legal foundation of the Federal government, and the congressional record does verify that. The Constitution gives the President the power to appoint judges with the advice and consent of the Senate. But the Constitution does NOT give the judges the power to turnaround and then appoint themselves as sovereign dictators over America with supreme authority even above God. This really is judicial abuse of power and outright tyranny! Not only that, Ms. Ginsburg is a former ACLU lawyer and favors their line of thinking. The ACLU is an anti-American, anti-God organization that is the equivalent of a large domestic terrorist cell determined to destroy American from within by attacking our most sacred rights and values. Just being a member of a radical group like the ACLU should have disqualified her from ever serving on the Court in the first place. And Stephen G. Breyer is part of the same pack of judges that believes his opinions supercede the law. That's otherwise known as power derived by the illegal, un-chartered, imaginary 'liquid constitution.' Mr. Breyer has claimed the Supreme Court Justices are the 'Moral Arbiters of America' and further thinks Supreme Court judges ARE the law. No they're NOT! The Constitution and the written laws of the various legislatures ARE the law. The judiciary is strictly an administrative department to judge whether or not the laws on the books have been broken. That's all a judge is suppose to do is judge. Judges have no Constitutional or legal grounds, or judicial authority to veto the rightful written laws, and substitute new rules or laws of their own. It's as simple as that! The Supreme Court has been out-of-order for a long time, and severely so for over fifty years, and it's high time we get it straightened out. That's what I'm doing, Helen." She might follow up with a comment like this—

"But you're out-of-order and abusing the separation of powers by eliminating Judges that the Constitution guarantees are appointed for life. Isn't that breaking the law? Can't you see you're making the Presidency out-of-order? And you've been out of order for some time, lying us into a war on falsified information, that ought to be an impeachable offense and ..."

Interrupting her the President might say, "Whoa! Whoa! Hold it right there! Somebody give a mirror to Helen so she can see what out-of-order looks like. This is a news conference, not a Bash Bush Seminar. Let's stick to the subject and quit professing the same old tired partisan lies about me lying us into the Iraq War.

You know perfectly well everybody had access to the same intelligence information, which was mostly compiled during the Clinton administration. Most of the Democrats who voted to go into Iraq, and claimed I gave them phony intelligence, publicly showed concern about Saddam having WMD's two years before I even took office. When my approval rating hit 92% after 911 they panicked because partisan politics and keeping their jobs is more important to them than patriotism, the welfare of the people or national security. So they suddenly schemed up the lie that I faked that intelligence. The truth is the Democrats are the ones who were lying!

Now uh.. getting back to the court situation— The Constitution doesn't say a single thing about Judges being appointed for life. It says they can keep their jobs during good behavior. That's the exact wording. Look it up for yourself, Article III section 1. Furthermore, it doesn't say a darn thing about separation of church and state either. That lie was the biggest judicial blunder in the history of America regarding Constitutional interpretation, and it led to the biggest moral decline of our country, too. But the Constitution does say the government, specifically congress, has no authority to prohibit the free exercise of religion, free speech, freedom of the press or the right of the people to peacefully get together to complain about government abuses of their liberties. Freedom! That's what the First Amendment is really all about.

It's NOT about separation. And it's not about establishment. The misunderstood establishment clause is a restriction only on the government, including the Supreme Court, to maintain a hands-off policy and not violate the peoples rights. I don't consider any Judge who doesn't respect the original purpose and intent of the real Constitution as being in good behavior. They're incompetent and unqualified to sit on the bench! And when they appoint themselves as sovereign dictators, that's serious tyranny!" Upon making this statement a rumble would fill the room and the President might field a question from the starkly handsome CNN correspondent, John Roberts, formerly of CBS news:

"Mr. President, I'm not sure any President has ever so boldly attacked Supreme Court Justices with such harsh rhetoric. Could we assume sir, that you have been brain-washed by the radical rightwing philosophies of the New Patriots of America? We know they've been bombarding the Whitehouse and Congress with their literature, e-mails and letters. Could you elaborate on that?" The President could answer:

"I'd be glad to. There's nothing radical or rightwing about common sense logic based on the truth. That's neither left nor right. It's right down the middle.. about as basic as understanding can get. That's where America started. We need people on the Supreme Court who understand American history. . . who understand the first group of Amendments were called the "Bill of Rights." Doesn't it make sense that those Amendments were all about protecting the RIGHTS of the people? So where do some Supreme Court judges get the idea the Bill of Rights allows the court to take the peoples rights away? A pre-school child can understand there's something severely wrong with that. We would have been better off if we'd had kindergarten kids running the court a few decades ago.

We've had some judges on the Supreme Court who didn't even understand the purpose and intent of the first half-sentence of the First Amendment which states, 'Congress shall make no law respecting an establishment of religion; or prohibiting the free exercise thereof.' Back in 1962 six judges on the court twisted those words around and declared they meant, 'This Constitution guarantees separation of Church and State.' No it doesn't! It means what it says! The judges back then must have been ignorant of our history relating to the American Revolution. The reason our Founding Fathers declared our independence from King George III of England was because of gross abuses of power. They didn't want the new American government to declare one Christian denomination as the official State Church like King George did with the Church of England. Let's get it straight once and for all.

The Bill of Rights is all about protecting the peoples rights. And our Founding Fathers considered the unalienable right to freedom of religion to be the most sacred and important of our rights. That's why it was the first thing addressed in the First Amendment. What it boils down to is this— we've had some rather incompetent judges on the Supreme Court and I'm determined to correct that. OK? uh.. next question.. uh George Stephanopoulos."

"Mister President, Supreme Court decisions since 1947 have upheld the legal ideology of 'separation of church and state.' How can you declare Judges of the High Court to be incompetent when they are just following the normal procedure of precedent, the legal concept of *stare decisis?* After all, citing legal precedent isn't something that is going to go away, even if certain justices could be removed from the court. In short, how can you justify putting a halt to an everyday common legal practice like precedent?"

"I don't know. How do you stop a dog from chasing it's tail? I guess we have to realize what's happening and just stop doing something that doesn't make sense, isn't getting us anywhere, and has us running in useless circles. And well, since Supreme Court decisions have been corrupt for about a half century I don't think precedent should ever be allowed again as a basis for deciding a court case. For one thing, we don't have to cite a court precedent in any case. That's the best answer to your question. However, I would like to point out that the Supreme Court never cited one reference of stare decisis when they declared the lie that the First Amendment means separation of Church and State. And the reason is, there were no previous cases declaring anything close to separation of Church and State.

Now uh.. You may be wondering how previous, and even some of our current Judges, could be so wrong about understanding the Constitution. Well,.. could it be they think they're elite because they're educated beyond their intelligence? That's my theory. They've cited emanations and penumbras as a cover-up excuse for discarding actual laws on the books and Constitutional wording in favor of making their personal opinions the law. Well, what are emanations and penumbras? Emanation means to originate. These outlaw judges are saying they have a right to originate the law. They are in the Judiciary Department. Their job is judicial administration, to uphold the laws that are written by Congress, and.. as I said before, to simply make a judgment as to whether or not those laws have been broken, not originate their own laws. That's what Judges are suppose to do, just judge. Congress is the legislative branch and the only government department, aside form Executive proclamations, authorized by the Constitution to be law-makers. And uh.. what are penumbras? I had to look that up in the dictionary myself. It means partial, grayish shadows. Hey! That's fuzzy thinkin' folks! The Constitution doesn't need to be interpreted by fuzzy thinkers on the Supreme Court who are fumbling around looking for meanings between the lines. We need people on the Court who have enough intelligence to look for meanings by reading and understanding the words. The Constitution is clearly written in English. It doesn't need to be interpreted, uh.. unless you're an illegal immigrant who hasn't learned the language yet."

-0-

After the news conference, the next day we could expect the following excerpt of propaganda from The New York Times—

This unprecedented action by the President followed his reading of a controversial book titled, *The U.S. Supreme Court is GUILTY!* This book organized conservative bigots throughout the nation, calling themselves the New Patriots of America, (the NPA) who bombarded the President and Capitol Hill with their insipid rhetoric for months, claiming the First Amendment in no way guarantees separation of Church and State. They've insisted it's not about separation. It's not about establishment. It's all about freedom for the people! The NPA has been unrelenting with their prejudiced dialogue claiming the First Amendment is about guaranteeing the most basic and most sacred rights we have as human beings. They claim that's why the Founding Fathers made protection of these rights the first Amendment, because these are the most important rights and the Constitution guarantees all citizens absolute freedom of religion, freedom of speech, freedom of the press and peaceful assembly for a redress of grievances, on every inch of American soil, including all government properties, and the NPA claims the highly misunderstood establishment clause is a restriction only on government to not violate, as they put it, 'the sacred rights of the people.' So goes the warped rhetoric of the New Patriots of America. We at The New York Times agree only with their zeal to maintain freedom of the press.

The next morning, former Secretary of Education and host of Salem Radio Network's "Morning in America," Bill Bennett, might say, "Throughout history revolutions traditionally have followed a prolonged period of some sort of abuse. Pressure slowly builds and then one day it explodes into a revolution. Do you agree, Seth? Seth would answer, "Absolutely! That's what happened yesterday. It's another example of the spirit to be free proving once again that America is the last great hope." Bill would have to say, "Where have I heard that before? Thank you Seth, but you don't have to plug my book again." Seth's likely reply, "I know where my bread is buttered, Sir!" Bill would respond, "Ha, ha, well.. Maureen from Cincinnati is on the line. Good morning Maureen!"

"Good morning Dr. Bennett. Well, this really is a great day in America! I'm so proud of our President for taking this stand for freedom and helping all Americans to understand one of the truths the New Patriots of America have clearly revealed, that there is no Constitutional grounds for separation of Church and State. It was a monumental judicial blunder on the part of incompetent Judges of the Supreme Court." Dr. Bennett probably would answer—

"At last the great lie has been overcome by the truth." 'Be Astute in the Truth. Deny the Lie."

"That was one of my favorite NPA slogans. But looking toward the next step. Do you think the Senate will give their consent?

"That's a good question, Maureen. It all depends on how effective the New Patriots of America movement has been in convincing the public and the Senators of the truth. We still need the votes of some Democrats to make it constitutionally official. It might be close. Then again, when you see all of the signs posted in peoples yards, and in so many church yards all over America, I think it's going to make the Democrats think twice about bucking public opinion only on the grounds of pure partisan politics. It would let the voters know Democrats really don't care about the good of the country or the rights of the people, that they are only interested in themselves and their political careers."

"Exactly! It would be so obvious they're doing it for political reasons, because they have no ethical or legal foundation to go against the President's stand."

"Let's hope the Democrats do something right for a change."

"But you know, Dr. Bennett, let's assume they do approve it, I'm wondering how this is going to affect our public education system. How long will it take to get the liberal teachers to allow an acknowledgement of God in the classroom? Many of our public educators have been brain-washed for a long period. A lot of them don't believe in God and are teaching our children liberal attitudes.

"Yes, but a lot of school administrators totally gave up on teaching the right things because they were afraid of the ACLU. If we can get the Supreme Court to declare separation of Church and State to be unconstitutional all of that will change for the better. I think you're right about the need to get God back in the educational system. I don't see how we can have a quality education without God, because God has played such a significant role in our nation's history. The continental army was losing. George Washington prayed and we won against overwhelming odds. The Constitutional Convention was deadlocked. Benjamin Franklin suggested the delegates pray and they received divine inspiration to construct the Constitution, which, in many ways, is a sacred document. As far as trying to speculate on a time table? It's hard to say. But one thing for sure, once the Supreme Court is back on track at least no one can be stopped from acknowledging God or praying and asking God's blessing on our country, the teachers and students. Columbine happened by kids getting the devil in 'em 'cause the Supreme Court took God out of the classrooms."

"I think you hit the nail on the head when you say it's how effective the truth is on our representation in Washington. You know what the good book says? We shall know the truth and the truth will set us free!"

"Amen to that. It'll be interesting to watch. Thanks for the call, Maureen."

-0-

The Laura Ingram Show is another outstanding syndicated conservative radio talk show heard throughout the country. How would Laura handle the news?

"Secretary Rumsfeld, it's an honor to have you on the show again and I don't care what anyone says I think you will go down in history as a most outstanding Secretary of Defense."

“Thank you, Laura. It’s always a pleasure to talk to you. I know you visited with our troops in Iraq, and I appreciate your candid exposure of the positive side in that conflict. I know our brave men and women serving in the military appreciated it, too.”

“A great deal was accomplished by our military presence, like the destruction of the Taliban in Afghanistan, and the end of two of the most inhumane dictatorships in history, the capture of Saddam Hussein, the destruction of his two sons and Al Zarqawi, confiscating countless caches of enemy equipment and weaponry, including some deadly WMD’s. To listen to the LIBERAL press you’d think the only thing that happened in Iraq was roadside bombs and a Civil War.”

“I know, Laura. Much of the unpatriotic news media never mentions the positive facts, such as— the Iraqi government being established in only three years while Al Qaida terrorists were a constant threat. You know, it took fifteen years for American patriots to come up with a workable government and ratify our Constitution after the American Revolution. And they weren’t threatened by terrorist activity. The vast majority of the Iraqi people were proud to be free to vote. Considering the contentions among the various theocratic groups there, what we accomplished was pretty phenomenal.”

“It is indeed. But I brought up the war effort only because Helen Thomas had to keep hitting on it at the President’s news conference yesterday. Aren’t you proud of the way President Bush defended himself?”

“I would say he won a big battle in the war to defeat a corrupt court system.”

-0-

The Washington Post would likely crank up their propaganda machine and print something like this—

The NPA has been touting the strange line of reasoning that the establishment clause of the First Amendment restricts only the government, (and they claim that includes the Supreme Court) from telling any citizen what to believe or how to worship or not worship. The NPA further claims that the Bill of Rights is a notice to representatives of the government to maintain a hands-off policy regarding the people's rights, and claims the First Amendment is every citizens guarantee that the United States government is founded on the principles to serve and respect the citizenry with an obligation to forever let the people be free. We at The Washington Post are appalled at the audacity of this intolerant, homophobic, sexist, imperialistic group insisting that the Constitution means exactly what it says, when we know it means what the Supreme Court says it means. For the last half-century the majority opinion of the Court says it means Separation of Church and State and therefore it might as well be carved in stone.

-0-

That afternoon the founder of conservative talk radio, Rush Limbaugh, would probably respond, "After the President's encounter with the Drive-By-Media taking pot shots at him, and any logical conservative thought, it was good to hear the echo of cannon fire blasting back at them. I've been tellin' ya all along folks, the Drive-By-Media was going to get their just due because their bias is not based on any sound doctrine. President Bush did a great job of defining true justice regarding the judiciary branch of government, standing up for everybody's rights to their own opinions, and making it clear tyrants in the courts don't have a right to tromp all over the hallowed rights of the people. Bush just told it like it is. Just straight forward honest to God truth about how wrong court decisions have been and how right and bright he's going to make the future. The Dem's and all the rest of the lib's are goin' nuts because they know a conservative court is going to literally put them out of business. Goodbye ACLU. Goodbye Planned Parenthood. Adios abortion slaughter houses. Eat your heart out Hillary and Bill. I'd like to sing it's been good to know ya, but it has been anything but. Although, I suppose it would only be appropriate to thank the Clintons for many delightful hours of liberal material to chop to shreds on the EIB Network. I wouldn't want to appear ungrateful for the Clinton's only real contribution to American society."

Also in the afternoon the Dennis Prager Show is heard on the Salem Radio Network.

"Hey Dennis, I'm a first time caller. I feel compelled to call 'cause I just had to get across a point that most everybody seems to have missed regarding Bush and the court. Don't you see he's trying to get in a cheap shot at the Supreme Court, to get back at them for their decisions against military tribunals at Guantanamo, and other decisions that put Bush in his place? Bush thinks he has a right to have a free hand to do whatever he wants, like he's some kind of king or somethin'.. and he's just fightin' the court 'cause they've been doin' a good job of cuttin' Bush down to size." Prager would probably answer—

"No, I don't think the President is acting vindictively at all. I think President Bush is trying to do what is right, in spite of those who want to do what's wrong."

"Come on Dennis. Bush is just attempting to fix his bad ratings in the polls, that's all."

"Sure the polls have gone up for the President's performance ratings since yesterday but he has made it clear many times he doesn't make decisions based on the polls. He makes decisions based on what he thinks is the right thing to do for the country in the long run. I thank you for the call, but I have to disagree with you completely. What did you say your name was?

"Uh.. Michael Moore in Hollywood."

"Oh!"

-0-

Speculation by all the liberal press and the Democrats would be at a fever pitch as they try to calculate how much damage has been done to their evil agenda by the NPA spreading the truth. They would wonder how many voters have had their minds warped by sound doctrine, and how many of their Democrat Party cohorts will cave-in to public opinion and vote for impeachment of liberal Judges if it comes down to that.

Popular radio & TV host Larry King might have Ted Kennedy as a guest on his secular-oriented program, and ask—"Senator Kennedy, what is your take on this unusual concept by the President to remove judges from the bench?

"This is the wrong action at the wrong time, just as Iraq was the wrong war at the wrong time. In fact Larry, this is the wrong President for the wrong time."

"Senator, there's a lot of talk about *Roe vs. Wade* being overturned if this action by the President is approved by the Senate. You have always fought for a woman's right to choice. How do you see the battle shaping up politically?"

"I will fight this to my dying day with every ounce of energy I can muster. I can't see why the majority of Americans would want it any other way. It's up to the woman to decide what to do regarding her own body, not the Supreme Court."

"Very good, Senator. But let me play the devil's advocate for the sake of conversation. Won't those who oppose your viewpoint claim that's been their position all along— that it's not the Supreme Court's place to allow abortion since the court first ruled that *Roe vs. Wade* is the law of the land?"

"Uh well,.. Now if the shoe ends up on the other foot, we have to think accordingly in order to defend the right to choice!"

"Good thinking, Senator. No wonder you've been in the Senate for so long. You're a quick thinker."

Who knows? Larry King might think Ted Kennedy is a quick thinker, but the truth is he's just like all the liberals who will flip flop sides on any issue in order to carry out their evil agenda.

-0-

And who knows? Tune the radio to another station in those possible future days and conservative talk show host, Michael Medved, might have Bill Clinton as his guest on the Salem Radio Network.

"President Clinton, you are well aware of the situation with President Bush requesting the resignation of two Supreme Court Justices. How do you think Hillary will respond to this? Do you think it increases her chances of being President?"

"I haven't conversed with Hillary about it, but I'm sure she feels the same way I do. This New Patriot idea of freedom for the people doesn't make sense. Why have freedom for the people if you're going to have government for the people? I mean, if the government is going to be given the power to rule, then the government has to dominate, and the Supreme Court is the rule of law and is the final authority in America as I have always understood it. That's why they named it the SUPREME Court. They are the Supreme authority."

"Well, that certainly makes no sense to me, Sir! And that's mainly because the Constitution really does NOT give the final authority of law to the Supreme Court. It extends judicial power to the court to settle cases, in law and equity, arising under the Constitution and the laws of the United States. The Constitution defines the court duties as basically upholding the laws to settle disputes, not to originate laws by judicial dictate. Over the years certain Supreme Court justices have ASSUMED POWERS they had no legal authority to take for themselves, either Constitutionally or by congressional law, or even by a writ or proclamation of the President. They have literally stolen the power of our democratic republic away from the people, and for all practical purposes, have declared themselves to be legal dictators of American making this country into an oligarchy instead of the democratic republic it was meant to be. How can the people be free if we have court judges overruling their elected representatives and dictating substitute laws? Don't you understand this?"

"If I don't understand what 'is' is, how do expect me to understand what 'this' is? Ha, ha. Just kidding! But I will say this. If the people are going to look the other way and let government officials play, more power to the government officials, I say. It worked for me."

"With all due respect, President Clinton, did it really work for you? Or were you simply deceived into thinking it worked? I would like to get your opinion on a somewhat related question. The NPA has taken a very conservative view of homosexuality and lesbian rights, which they refer to as being a matter of sexual disorientation. One of the first actions you took during your term in office was to come out in favor of homosexuals in the military. Do you think the NPA is too harsh on this issue?

"Well, of course. Let's face it, we have to admit homosexuals and lesbians exist and respect their rights to exist, because they can't help who they are and the way they desire to live."

"On the contrary, Sir there are those who say we can all help who we are by respecting the natural laws of nature and common sense decency, rather than giving in to the unnatural lowest desires of the humanity that dwells here.. in this greatest nation on God's green earth."

-0-

If President Bush were to act on his Constitutional authority to begin ridding the nation of the judges of bad behavior it would continue to spark very heated debate throughout the conservative and liberal news media. We might expect to read an editorial in the Los Angeles Times quite similar to this:

The Bush administration has once again gone completely out-of-control in an unprecedented attempt to assume power a President was never meant to have. This foolish move is outrageous and runs contrary to everything we know to be politically correct. Hollywood stars over the years have set a standard everyone admires to which the popularity of Hollywood celebrities attests.

Following the ancient philosophies outlined by the antiquated thinking expressed by the New Patriots of America will set this nation, and the world, back two hundred years. How can they dare to expect people to go back to less desirable times and ignore the progress elite Supreme Court justices have accomplished by more finely tuning the First Amendment to mean separation of church and state, which has become a sacred judicial cow in modern American culture. How could they be so ignorant as to not respect modern science in regard to evolution? Any fool knows scientists have all of the answers to explain how we evolved to what we are today without any evidence of some imaginary invisible god's help.

How could anyone have the audacity to come out against harmless homosexuals, lesbians and transsexuals after they have come out of the closet and attained such love and admiration for their struggle to achieve equality and acceptance by practically the entire world? The NPA talks of rights and freedoms, but how can they be so primitive as to not recognize the right of a woman to be free to abort a simple accident of nature that might be a threat to the woman's health? The truth is they must be a species of people who haven't quite evolved enough from the ape stage. Perhaps if they watched more movies by such award-winning directors as Michael Moore they would be better educated to live in these modern times.

-0-

In the following days Fox TV News commentator, Bill O'Reilly, might present an editorial opinion on The O'Reilly Factor such as this— "The 'Secular Progressive' is a strange looking animal that is headed for the same fate as the Dodo bird, and it will become extinct for the same reason. These strange birds flock together under the same premise of protection, namely being too stupid to recognize who the enemy is. They have decided to be friends to those who are out to destroy them, as well as America and Israel. They fail to understand al Qaida is not a signer of the Geneva Convention, and therefore not subject to the protections of members who have signed the trusty old treaty, which is actually a legal contract all members agreed to as the rules for them conducting war amongst themselves on an equally ethical basis that is on a plane a little more humane than unbridled ruthless barbarism. Extending Geneva Convention protections to animals who are the most brutal, dirty, underhanded, back-stabbing, maiming, beheading, blood-thirsty, barbaric, crawly-creatures who ever drew breath, and are totally disrespectful of any form of human decency, is an indication the secular progressives and Dodo birds are truly birds of the same feather. Thank God we have a President who recognizes stupidity below the Dodo bird mentality is not a qualification for judges to continue to serve on the Supreme Court."

-0-

What might the future hold as we tune in conservative talk show host Hugh Hewitt:

"Randy, listening on 'The Patriot' in St. Paul, Minnesota.. you're on the Hugh Hewitt program! What's your view on the President's Supreme Court move?"

"I think it's great! A move in the right direction for sure. But I don't see why the President can't just simply fire judges without getting the approval of the Senate if they're guilty of things like incompetence, abuse of power and tyranny."

"That's an excellent point. But if a judge protests his firing could he try to sue the President on some trumped up grounds to get his job back? And how do you give a judge on the highest court in the nation his day in court? Who or what court would hear the case? Or would the Senate, with the President presiding as judge, become the court for an accused Supreme Court judge? It's like opening a legal can of worms. I don't know that there is a provision for such a circumstance in the wording of the Constitution or laws of Congress other than impeachment. Then you're back to more involvement of the Senate. It's a very interesting question Randy. I'm not sure anyone has an answer to it, right now."

"Well, if a company president hires somebody, he has the right to fire the guy if he does a poor job. If the President has the authority to appoint judges why can't he fire a judge who doesn't measure up to the requirement standards of the job, and on top of that, actually commits a crime? Abuse of power, and tyranny! Aren't those criminal acts?"

"It's certainly criminal from a moral standpoint, however I'm not sure there is a law on the books that defines what has been going on with the Supreme Court for years as tyranny or abuse of power. However, the Constitution does mention treason, and it also says that all criminal trials except impeachment shall be by jury."

"They need to work on some way for judges in the court system to be fired for poor or gross performance. For instance, what about the other three inept judges on the Supreme Court who haven't been asked to resign? I think the President should ask them to resign, too. We shouldn't have any bad judges on the court."

"No doubt you mean Anthony Kennedy, John Paul Stevens and David Souter. Yes! I believe they should and will eventually be asked to resign, along with a whole list of Federal judges on the Circuit Courts, and it should continue on down to each State court system. One that comes to mind is Judge Reinhart on the Ninth Circuit. These judges are as a much of a threat to the integrity of our moral values and national security as any who have served on the Supreme Court. Maybe someday they will focus on a law or Constitutional Amendment to remove bad judges, but for now I believe the President has done the right thing by asking for their resignations, because it allows them to be removed from the bench with their retirement benefits and avoids the ugly scene of impeachment."

"But another circumstance that could occur is, if a liberal Democrat eventually is elected President, couldn't that President reverse the process, because his values are reversed, and start eliminating conservative judges from the court?"

"I'm glad you brought that up, because the liberals would certainly want to do just that. However, President Bush has done the right thing by using Constitutional law as the authority for his actions and pointing out that Judges who substitute their own opinions in place of the legal written wording of the Constitution are outside the law and completely out-of-order and guilty of incompetence, abuse of power and tyranny."

"In other words, a future Supreme Court Judge who comes under attack by a liberal President, or a liberal member of Congress could stand on the Constitution for his defense."

"Exactly! The liberals would have to have a whole new Constitutional Convention and rewrite the Constitution to legally change the court back to the evils of liberal thinking. Excellent call. Thanks for checking in, Randy!"

-0-

So much for an interesting glimpse, through the magic of imagination, of a possible future if Americans will just get busy, stand up against judicial abuse and demand their rights as originally determined by our Founding Fathers. Now back to the hard truth of reality—

If we don't act quickly enough to get this movement rolling to influence both Democrats and Republicans before President Bush leaves office, we must vote a President and Congress into office in 2008 that will get it done.

Wake up America! Wake up!

It only took a handful of incompetent, misguided, unprincipled Supreme Court Judges to misunderstand the Constitution, and its protections of freedom for the people to cause the greatest moral decline in the history of the United States. And it will only take a few good people to make it right again. **In fact, it will only take one person to begin the process of rectifying the corrupt court decisions of the past half century. We must reveal to the President that the Constitution gives him the authority to take action to rid the courts of the judges of bad behavior.**

The rest of this book outlines what actions on the part of American citizens we need to take to start another American Revolution— this time for the Revival of our unalienable God-given rights to Freedom of Religion, Freedom of Speech and Freedom of the press. We must exercise our right to peaceful assembly for a redress of grievances and insist the government, including the courts, respect and restore our rights.

If the majority of Judges on the Supreme Court and the Federal Circuit Courts understood the principles of liberty for the people, and respected the righteousness of God as our Founding Fathers applied it to our government, America would not be in the moral decline we suffer with today. Many people are rushing to compose and pass Amendments to the Constitution in order to legally overrule corrupt court decisions. But consider this— Since the out-of-order judges of bad behavior illegally believe their opinions supercede the Constitution and the written laws, they could simply say any Amendment that is passed by Congress, even if properly ratified by three-fourths of the States, is UN-constitutional because the majority decisions of the judges are the law, not the written Constitution. And where would that leave us?

Right back where we started. The problem is not the Constitution. The problem is the out-of-control Judges! The problem is the incompetent liberal activist-tyrants who are abusing the power of the courts. It will be much faster and easier to remove Judges from the bench than it would be to ever get even one amendment added to the Constitution. It takes years to add an Amendment. Judges can be removed quickly. Once we subtract the Judges who are guilty of bad behavior we won't need to add many Amendments.

The Constitution states judges can keep their jobs during good behavior. The first step in our plan of action is to remove any Judges from any court that are guilty of bad behavior, who is so incompetent as to NOT understand and uphold the freedoms and rights the Constitution guarantees to We The People. Since the Constitution gives the President power to appoint Judges to the courts with the advice and consent of the Senate, it means the President can reduce the number of Judges, or ask for the resignation of any Judge on the basis of bad behavior, or threaten them with impeachment because of their incompetence, abuse of power and/or tyranny. This is precisely what God showed me we can do before I began writing this book, that the authority to eliminate unqualified Supreme Court Justices is in the legal wording of the Constitution. We don't have to wait for them to decide to retire or die to replace them. We just need to get busy and act now! Of course, the minute this revelation begins to circulate on Capitol Hill it will cause absolute pandemonium and heated debate.

Chapter 7

Founding the New Patriots of America

If you are moved in your heart to want to do something to correct the moral degradation, caused by a corrupt court system, that is denying and threatening the original ideals, rights and liberties set forth by the Founding Fathers of America, then join with others who believe the time has come for decent Americans everywhere to stand up and declare themselves to be the New Patriots of America! Who are the New Patriots of America? The following Charter helps to define us:

The New Patriots of America Charter

The New Patriots of America agree to declare a New American Revolution to legally strive for the revival of our God-given unalienable rights that the original Patriots fought the American Revolutionary War to secure, and proclaimed in the Declaration of Independence, the Constitution of the United States and the Bill of Rights. We are simply people with true morality who believe the original core values of this nation were right, and still believe that America should always be as it was in the beginning— One Nation Under God, with Liberty and Justice for all. New Patriots are no different than the original Patriots who wrote those revered historical documents upholding the basic principle that governments should be instituted to serve the people, uphold the venerated liberties of the people, and never trample upon the people's sacred God-given unalienable rights to freedom of religion, freedom of speech, freedom of the press, and freedom to peacefully correct the corruption of tyranny should any government officials forget the people are the final power and authority in a democratic republic. We believe the power belongs to the people, and our government exists to serve the people, that we are to be a free people, not slaves of the State. We are proud to be among those who stand for higher ideals and the sound principles of the Creator who put all things together, and also designed the order of its purpose, a purpose to preserve good above evil, to cherish love above hate, and with God's help to defeat the foes of freedom. The New Patriots of America are dedicated to keeping America the land of the free and the home of the brave, where every branch of the government must— Let the People be free!

-0-

The New Patriots of America is NOT a political party. It is NOT a religion. It is simply the organization of people of faith and moral values who are determined to keep our elected representatives aware of our desire to resurrect and preserve the original virtues that inspired the Founding Fathers to establish America as a free nation. We do not send people to Washington and State Capitols, or even County and City councils, for the purpose of serving themselves and making a career out of playing politics. The New Patriots of America want politicians to know they are elected for the purpose of being statesmen-like servants of We the People, and to do what is right in the eyes of God for the whole nation, not just their little corner of it. Anyone can claim to be a member of The New Patriots of America who believes in the principles of the NPA Charter and the NPA Declaration of Dependence on God. These documents fully define those who have the integrity to boldly acknowledge God, the principles of our Founding Fathers, and have the courage to uphold the Judeo-Christian heritage of America, with a determination to revive our precious liberties and revolt against those forces of evil destroying our heritage. Just as the original Patriots of America set forth their desires for liberty from the abuses of King George III of England by the Declaration of Independence, The New Patriots of America set forth their desires for liberty from the abuses of the Judicial Department of our government by the Declaration of Dependence on God.

The New Patriots of America

Declaration of Dependence on God

A Reclamation of the People's Rights by the Power of the Word

***We**, the New Patriots of America, following the example of the Founding Patriots of America, do solemnly and boldly declare the righteousness of Almighty God as the guiding enlightenment for our nation. We acknowledge our Dependence upon the one true Creator of the Heavens and the Earth, who is the source of our origin, provision, protection and eternal joy. We acknowledge that this nation was founded on His principles that bring blessings upon this land, and that His followers are commissioned to be the Salt of the Earth and the Light of the World. We believe it was in respect to God's authority that the Constitution owes its birth of rule, law and order.*

We further proclaim the Founding Fathers of America owe no one an apology for their faith, and were correct to build this nation on absolute Judeo-Christian values, and that no person, organization, nation, government or judicial body can rightfully claim our sacred heritage to be wrong, invalid or outdated.

We uphold the fact that certain inalienable rights are always correct, that among these are life, liberty and the pursuit of happiness, which includes the government respecting the precious rights of all individuals to enjoy complete religious freedoms, to be able to freely think, believe and worship as they see fit with complete impunity, while respecting the free will of those who choose not to do so with complete impunity. And that these liberties include the right of all citizens to be free to openly express their opinions and beliefs in a peaceful and orderly fashion, both privately and publicly, including in all Governmental chambers and properties, with no Governmental censorship, restriction or punishment of the free expression of decent thoughts and beliefs in speech or the printed word.

We recognize this truth— that the United States Constitution does NOT guarantee any degree of "Separation of Church and State," but that the First Amendment restrains only government from interfering with the free exercise of religion, while restricting only the government from establishing a State controlled Church. Therefore, we hold this truth to be self-evident; that the Church has every right and patriotic obligation to participate in every phase of the political process to control the Government, upholding the highest ideals of the heritage our Founding Fathers defined in the Declaration of Independence, the Constitution of the United States, The Bill of Rights and personal guidance from the Holy Scriptures.

We further state that whenever any form of government becomes destructive of these ends, disrespecting the principle of deriving their just powers from the consent of the governed while usurping the rights of the People against their will, it is the right and duty of the People to alter such governmental tyranny by unifying in prayer, fasting, engaging legal actions, impeachment, new legislation and the power of the vote.

We present the crimes of the U. S. Supreme Court and subsequent courts to be a history of repeated abuses of power and usurpations of the will of the People and the Congress, all having the direct effect of absolute Tyranny over these United States. To prove this, let the facts be submitted to a candid world:

The Justices have taken for themselves powers they were never meant to have, egotistically deciding their personal opinions supercede the opinions of the People, the People's elected representation in Congress, the Executive branch of the Federal Government and State Governments, ruling that only their opinions are "The Law of the Land," thereby turning America from a Democratic Republic into an Oligarchy. We will not tolerate the destruction of democracy in America by a government with ultimate power vested in a few un-elected officials.

They have been the friend of crime and criminals, and those who defend crime and criminals professing ungodly, un-American attitudes, while ignoring common decency and the traditional sacred moral values and rights of the law-abiding citizenry. They have handicapped law enforcement officials by respecting criminal's rights, ruling that legal procedures supercede justice, favoring the guilty, while showing little regard for the rights of the law-abiding citizens, or what is truly right or wrong.

They have denied public school children any rights to the acknowledgement of God's existence, authority and virtues, while upholding the lie of evolution; thereby they are GUILTY of contributing to endless counts of juvenile delinquency and several generations of ever-declining moral standards. We note that education devoid of God is learning devoid of high values.

They have committed judicial treason, taking an oath to uphold the Constitution and laws of the United States while harboring disrespect and contempt for the Constitution, the laws of Congress, and the various States by overstepping their own jurisdiction to make decisions based on laws, political or social attitudes of foreign nations. We profess that foreign ways of worldly thinking are not necessarily the ways of Godly virtue.

They have accepted the lower standards of other regions of the world to strike down our long-standing laws against perverted and unnatural lifestyles, encouraging this abominable behavior and those who practice it, who seek to further corrupt the sanctity of marriage while claiming intolerance of their desires is a hate crime, and the Bible is a hate book. Let it be clear that tolerance of evil is no act of love. The claim for tolerance in this case is a deceitful act of Satan to silence God's will to save those who are headed for destruction. No one is born to be evil, and even if they are deceived enough to think so, they can still be spiritually born again! Those who practice unnatural love don't need their lustful sensuality. They need God's loving salvation!

The judges of our courts quote "Freedom of Speech" as the legal basis to protect filth and pornography, but deny true freedom of speech in regard to the expression and display of the right to the free exercise of religion.

Certain Justices of the High Court have innocent blood on their hands for the slaughter of many millions of unborn babies in America since the decision of Rowe vs. Wade. God recognizes fetuses as living souls saying, "I knew you when you were still in your Mother's womb." May God have mercy on our nation for these heinous crimes that are mostly the result of very low promiscuous moral standards protected by rulings of the Court. We observe that if young single women would make the choice to endorse God's pure and righteous ways, the vast majority of them would never have to make a choice regarding abortion.

The Justices have committed the high crime of showing blatant contempt, not only for the Declaration of Independence and the Constitution of the United States, but for the sacred honor and moral values of the original Patriots who, under the inspiration of Almighty God, drafted those documents following prayers for His guidance. The court demeans all Americans who fought and died to defend our religious liberties. In so doing, the Court is GUILTY of a gross lack of patriotism paramount to treason, inciting a need for sedition to express our grievances.

The U.S. Supreme Court and the entire jurisprudence system has been tainted and corrupted by evil reasoning, and intentions aligned with the Forces of Darkness. They have established atheism and other false and secular doctrines of belief as the only legal religious beliefs respected by our government, thereby becoming the core cause of discrimination against the highest and holiest principles of God, His followers and the heritage of this nation. We must correct them, reminding these judges the Constitution does NOT indicate our government must be Godless, and separated from His virtuous principles.

The Court has enormously erred by mocking the truth of God's existence and authority, insulting God by striking down public acknowledgement of our heritage in Him, interfering greatly and unjustly with the free exercise of religion. They are GUILTY of arrogant despotism, claiming their personal opinions to be "a super legislature," and "the sole arbiter of our nation's moral standards" therefore setting themselves above the will of the People and even God's supremacy. We proclaim they are NOT to rule as dictatorial gods of America. They have become a blaspheming affront to God, His righteousness, and those who uphold His righteousness. They have no right to take God's place in our lives.

We point to the fact that the Supreme Court was established by Article III of the Constitution of the United States, which defines it as "The Judicial Department," NOT a legislating branch of government. Their job is NOT to determine what the law is to be, but to determine if the laws as written have been broken or not. We officially declare certain Justices of the Court, over many years, to be GUILTY of tyranny, grossly overstepping their jurisdictional authority.

The Courts have even violated the basic principles of the preamble to the Constitution, making a mockery of true justice, dividing the nation instead of insuring domestic tranquility, weakening the common defense, degrading the general welfare, and threatening the blessings of liberty to ourselves and our posterity that the Framers of the Constitution ordained for all of us to enjoy.

Enough is enough! To be tolerant of evil is no virtue! We recognize all of mankind is engaged in a Spiritual War. We will not be deceived. We declare we will no longer tolerate an evil oligarchy as supreme over America.

To the contrary, the New Patriots of America are humbly dedicated to acknowledging Almighty God as the Supreme Judge over us and our Nation. We pledge our allegiance to His name, the name above all names, the Lord of lords and King of kings, to whom is given all authority over the Heavens and the Earth. We are not ashamed of the gospel of Jesus Christ, nor should anyone claim to be offended by it, for He is the greatest thing that ever happen to humanity. He paid the price for the sins of all mankind with His compassionate sacrifice on the cross. For God so loved the world, that He gave His only begotten Son, that whosoever believes in Him shall not perish, but have ever-lasting life. No one goes to the Father but by Him. Jesus is every person's only eternal saving grace, if we will but accept His most magnificent free gift of eternal life.

We acknowledge it is God's truth that sets us free. With the same resolve as the original Patriots who founded our nation, we affirm faith in Divine Providence to overcome evil with good, reclaiming America as truly the land of the free and the home of the brave, where we will once again enjoy the total free exercise of religion. We accept this awesome responsibility with malice toward none, for Christ commands we love our enemies. He also said, "By this shall all men know that you are my disciples, if you have love one for another." We battle not against our fellow brothers and sisters, but against the evil deceit of the demonic principalities and powers that blind them and bind them.

Let us boldly march forward in this spiritual battle to Reclaim America for Christ, proclaiming God's righteousness, love, forgiveness, mercy and grace to guide us as we pray for the judges of America, that they may see the righteousness and glory of God's light, and repent of their evil ways and feeble incompetence. But if the hearts of the Judges remain hardened, we must stage a determined counter-attack and insist upon their resignations or demand impeachment.

The Signers of this Declaration support the battle to win the Great American Spiritual Revolution. We, the New Patriots of America, firmly and diligently declare our Dependence on God will bring us victory, for greater is He who is in us, than he who is in the world. We diligently uphold and defend our inalienable God-given rights, and demand that our government ***Let the People be Free!***

-0-

Some people will be inspired by the previous document because they know that, whether we realize it or not, every human being on this earth is engaged in a spiritual war which is now leading up to the end times. If you are inspired to do something to help bring about the Revolution for the Revival of our Constitutional God-given rights, then you have chosen to be on God's side in this spiritual struggle. Such a revolution will also bring about a Spiritual Revival of respect for God and the saving of lost souls. The people have been complacent and in the dark for too long. Will you help to enlighten them? We only need a small percentage of dedicated people of action who will help educate the populace and motivate our leaders, in order to cause millions to be sympathizers and supporters of this worthwhile cause.

Join in the work of the New Patriots of America (NPA)

To become a New Patriot, all you have to do is to proclaim you *are* one. Tell your family members, your friends and associates you are one of the New Patriots of America and encourage them to join this movement to save our nation from political and judicial tyranny. There are no absolute required obligations, other than to be sympathetic to the cause and act accordingly. You don't have to start an NPA Chapter in you area or join a group, but you can if you want. Those who truly want to make real changes in the betterment of American society are encouraged to get involved and be leaders in this movement. You don't have to take a pledge or sign anything, but you can if you desire. You might want to sign a copy of The New Patriots of America Declaration of Dependence on God. You can do so on line. Simply go to our website at www.newpatriotsofamerica.org. There is no membership card to carry around, but there could be someday. You don't have to wave a flag, but it's good to honor "Old Glory" and there is an NPA flag design with the outside corners rounded so that when it is raised the pole and flag forms the silhouette of the Letter "P" when the wind blows to the "Right." There is no membership fee or dues to pay, nor will there be acceptance of any donations, but you can spend your own money to personally promote the cause if you so desire, although such appropriations would NOT be tax deductible. (An explanation for this is outlined on the next few pages).

The New Patriots of America will strive for passage of legislation to insure our rights and freedoms are guaranteed. One such piece of legislation is a bill to be introduced as a congressional law until it can be passed as an Amendment to the Constitution. It's The Will of the People Act. If, in the future, a decision by the Supreme Court is handed down that is as unpopular, by a vast majority of the people, as those relating to separation of church and state, abortion, same-sex marriage and similar decisions, The Will of the People Act will give the people a means to exercise their authority as the final power in this democratic republic to overrule dictatorial judges and live according to the will of the citizenry. In other words, on issues of great importance, the majority will of the people should prevail as the last say in how a free society lives. The purpose and intent of a law should be clearly and simply defined so that lawyers, judges and juries would have no doubts about it in order to prevent a misuse or circumvention of the law. It should not be easy to repeal a Supreme Court decision, but it should not be impossible either. We the people who have to live with decisions of the court should have some means to be able to check and balance the power of our government leaders so that tyranny and government abuse can be prevented. With that in mind, the following is a suggestion for wording of the Will of the People Act:

The Will of the People Act

The purpose and intent of this law is to insure that the United States of America should always remain as a democratic republic, not an oligarchy, with final approval of issues concerning the rights of the people to be determined by consent of the governed, that is— by a vote of the people's representation in government, rather than a court judgment. Proposals to repeal a decision of the Supreme Court and/or Federal Circuit Courts may become law by a majority vote of both Houses of Congress with approval by the Executive Department, plus ratification by a simple majority of the legislatures of the various States.

-0-

Once the U.S. Supreme Court and Circuit Courts are cleaned up and are dominated by Justices who respect the written law as the legal rule of law, rather than Justices who want to rule by their personal dictates, we will be able to pass the Will of the People Act without any members of the judiciary claiming it is unconstitutional. The Will of the People Act will accomplish what it is designed to do, namely to prevent America from being ruled as an oligarchy by a small committee of un-elected judges or a single Circuit Court judge. This, of course, represents a major shift of the final legal power and authority of the United States, from the tyranny of illegal stealing of power by previous judges of bad behavior, giving power to the free people who have the right to final approval of the laws by which they will live and abide in a democratic republic. This was the original purpose and intent of establishing and operating the United States government. The government exists to serve us and let the people be free, not to enslave us and force us to obey the warped opinions of an un-elected few. If Judges had not engaged in judicial abuse, none of this would have been necessary.

Approval by both houses of Congress with the signature of the President, plus ratification by a simple majority of the State legislatures, makes it more difficult to change a decision of the Judiciary than simply passing a law, but makes it somewhat easier than adding an Amendment to the Constitution. This law provides a necessary check to assure the balance of power will maintain America as a free nation with final power in the hands of the people.

Some will argue and object to this on the grounds that if the people become corrupt the laws might become corrupt. True! But if the majority of the voting public becomes corrupt there will be little hope for the survival of that society anyway. However, when the court has already been corrupt for over a half century in such a way as to greatly proliferate the corruption of society it is time to act NOW to correct this atrocity! To further safeguard our freedoms and the balance of power, we should then strive to convert the Will of the People Act into the form of a Will of the People Amendment to the Constitution to further lock down the rights of the citizenry of this free society.

Another law the NPA should strive to pass in Congress, and go on to add as a Constitutional Amendment in order to rein-in the out-of-order court system, is The Judicial Jurisdiction Act. This law would place limits and boundaries on the authority of the Judicial branch of our government. Suggested wording for this document is as follows:

The Judicial Jurisdiction Act

The purpose and intent of this law is to clarify that the United States judiciary system is a judicial administrative department of government with the responsibility of upholding the legal laws written by the legislatures, and not a department with power to originate laws. The only judicial review allowed by Justices of the Supreme Court, and all subsequent Courts of the United States, are hereby limited to making judgments and decisions based only on the literal wording of the United States Constitution, the legally written laws of the U. S. Congress and the written laws of the various legislatures and law-making councils and governments within the States. Judges are to uphold these laws and make case decisions as to whether or not the written laws have been violated or not, with no judge handing down a decision based on personal opinions that are contrary to the legally ratified wording of the written laws on the books. Anyone charged with a crime has the right to request the court judge to cite aloud the written law or laws applicable to the case. No judge shall declare a law to be unconstitutional unless the wording of the law is clearly contrary to the wording of the Constitution or active legislated laws, in which case the court should request the responsible legislature to clarify, reword or otherwise change the law, with the exception of laws specifically written to repeal a former law.

-0-

The Judicial Jurisdiction Act (that could also possibly be a future Constitutional Amendment) is legislation needed to prevent judicial abuse of power in the future and allow for correction of past abuses.

The Call to Action

Here is the Plan of Action in a capsule to revive our rights and get America back on track. First we must get the President to ask for the resignations of unqualified Judges on the court. Once we have a Supreme Court with a majority opinion that respects the Constitution and the written laws of Congress as the true laws of the land, and declares many of the Supreme Court decisions of the past half century to be illegal blunders by unqualified, incompetent Judges, the evils that plague us will begin to fall like dominoes. First should come clearing up the falsehood of separation of Church and State. When this phony concept is revealed as the great flawed judicial error it is, and is declared unconstitutional, it will create the return of a moral America as it was in the beginning, one nation under God. No devil has a right to separate our government from God, or to separate people of faith from the free exercise of religion, or freedom of speech, or acknowledging God on government property. Demonic organizations such as the ACLU will be unable to win another case to destroy our rights to freedom of religion, adding insult to injury by abusing civil rights laws to force the tax-payers to foot the bill for court costs. This will put the ACLU and many other anti-American, anti-God organizations, such as Americans United for Separation of Church and State, out of business and make them legally impotent and ineffective to ever again intimidate the innocent people who want to exercise their Constitutional right to freedom of religion, freedom of speech and freedom of the press.

Equally important is the overthrowing of the court decision regarding *Roe vs. Wade* in order to halt the massive murder of the helpless and innocent. This will force the closing of most of the abortion slaughter houses in America. And it will force responsible adults to teach young people to be more moral and restrain from fornicating and engaging in loose moral standards outside of marriage which cause so many unwanted pregnancies. After that, good judges will be able to overturn all of the decisions of judges of bad behavior as we bring cases before them to accomplish this goal.

Steps to take to Revive our Freedoms

The following is a brief outline of *A Plan of Action* to guarantee a relatively quick turnaround of our judicial system and only allow Judges of high values and integrity on the bench.

ORGANIZE A NEW PATRIOTS OF AMERICA CHAPTER- Anyone who is excited about changing and improving the moral fiber of society in this country can organize a chapter of New Patriots of America by simply using two simple tools— this book and the NPA website www.newpatriotsofamerica.org. This book can easily serve as a manual of information and instruction and will tell you what activities to pursue to organize concerned citizens on your block, in your town, county or State into an effective group determined to change things for the better in America. The website can act as a cost-effective way to communicate with others and quickly spread the word to family, friends and associates. Your chapter can consist of only you and those you interest in this movement, and exist as strictly an internet chapter with members anywhere in the world. Or it can consist of people in your immediate neighborhood, town, city or county who enjoy getting together to discuss ways to raise money to print materials, or to work on various activities to accelerate a return to an America in which we can once more be proud to live.

The NPA is NOT a political party. It is NOT a religious church-sponsored organization. And it is not incorporated as a non-profit organization. No tax-deductible donations will be solicited or accepted in order to stay free of any government control or penalties by the Internal Revenue Service which underhanded politicians or others opposed to this movement could attempt to exploit in order to squelch the activities and purposes of the NPA. **I have founded The New Patriots of America as an information source to enlighten Americans to the truth so we can influence our political leaders to act on our behalf, to preserve our sacred rights and to do what is right for the good of the nation.** What makes this movement exciting is the fact that with just a few active concerned citizens we can make a huge difference toward turning things around in a relatively short period of time. To be successful in reviving our rights The New Patriots of America only need to be a voting block of "Values Voters" large enough to swing an election. Then all politicians will not be able to ignore us. The NPA can have a leadership of only a handful of people but have a following of 30 or 40-million or more. That is not an unrealistic evaluation. Read on for a basic list of activities to help us reach our goals. Perhaps you can think of more. Your input could be very effective and valuable to the cause.

PRAY FERVENTLY- The first step is to humble ourselves and call out to God in prayer. This is something every person can do. There is great power in fervent prayer. God can change things we can't. He can change peoples hearts and minds by driving out demonic forces that influence a person's feelings, their thinking and loyalty. Christ said, "You have not, because you ask not. Ask and you shall receive. Believe you'll receive what you pray for and you shall have it. Seek and you shall find. Knock and it shall be opened unto you." PRAY! PRAY, PRAY for God's help to pour out His Spirit to revive America as truly the land of the free, a land of responsible people exercising their freedom of religion and expression of beliefs.

PRAY FOR THE PRESIDENT- Pray that the President will be enlightened, and realize we have the legal answer to getting rid of the evils that plague our land in the wording of the Constitution, by getting rid of the judges of bad behavior in our court system. **Pray that the President will be inspired to stand up for the people's First Amendment rights. Pray that the President will see that he has the Constitutional power to ask for the resignation of incompetent judges of bad behavior. <u>This action by the President, with consent of the Senate, is the simple key to the success of this revolution for the revival of our rights</u>. Pray that members of the Senate will see the light to do what is right.** In order to accomplish our goal, and muster the votes needed in the Senate, it will be necessary to make an impact on public opinion and take part in other actions listed here.

COMMUNICATE WITH THE WHITE HOUSE— Stand up and be counted. Let the President know you're concerned about your unalienable rights being denied by incompetent, unqualified Judges in our court system whose bad decisions are being taken advantage of by the greedy ACLU that works to destroy our liberties. Encourage him by sending a simple letter, post card or e-mail, or make a phone call to the White House (202) 456-1111 and leave a brief message. Do at least one of these things once a week, and encourage others to do the same to **make sure the President understands the importance of restoring our most sacred rights that many patriots fought and died to preserve.** Let's make sure they have not died in vain. Make the President aware of what has been covered in this book as a source of information and a comprehensive understanding of the enemy that is destroying America from within. A few people may want to send him a copy of this book to make sure he gets the message.

FLOOD CONGRESS WITH CORRESPONDENCE– It's very important to let your Senators and Congressmen know about your concern also. Look up the e-mail addresses of your Federal Congressmen and Senators and contact them. Keep a constant stream of requests flowing to them asking them to support the idea to clean up the Federal court system. Then start contacting your State representatives. And don't just contact Republicans; it's just as important, if not more so, to let Democrats know it's for the good of the country as a whole for them to abandon their extreme leftist liberal leanings, show some patriotism, move back to the middle and unite with their fellow Americans for the good of our society and to strengthen our national defense. But don't be fooled by the Democrat Party strategy of putting up a false front of being moderate or conservative at election times. They have been experts at deceit in the past. The real test of their sincerity and integrity is how they vote on the issues after elected, especially when it comes to approving judges for the court system. This goes for Republicans, too. Let them know your concerns. Remember, politicians need our votes to keep their jobs. They want to know what the voters think. So let them know by methods suggested in this book or any way you can. And let those court judges of bad behavior know you are praying for them to wake up and see the light before they lose their jobs because of their tyrannical, abusive attitudes.

GET PETITIONS SIGNED- Gather names on petitions, either door to door or on-line, to present to the President and Congress, as well as the Supreme Court Justices themselves. A statement to present to signers might be the following—

"I agree with the Founding Fathers of our nation, and my fellow New Patriots of America, that the United States Supreme Court and various subsequent courts of the Federal government were never meant to reign as the supreme authority over these United States of America. And further declare that our country was meant to be a Democratic Republic with supreme authority in the hands of free people ruled by the Constitution of the United States, and the laws written by the people's representatives in Congress, the various legislatures, and proclamations of the executive branch, and that the courts are to uphold those laws and proclamations, never to invent laws of their own to rule over 'We the People' as un-elected dictators. I proclaim the 'Bill of Rights' was ratified for the purpose of our government always guaranteeing those rights to the people, with no court, or any other department of government denying any of our sacred rights and liberties."

Encourage celebrities, many sports personalities, politicians and others to do public service announcements requesting all concerned Americans to sign a petition and get involved in restoring our rights.

LET'S ADVERTISE OUR DESIRE FOR FREEDOM- A big part of the problem of correcting the horrible mistakes and tyrannies of the Supreme Court is that most people haven't gotten the message because the deceived liberal press is busy producing propaganda that favors the evil side of the issues. We need a massive advertising campaign to get the message across, to get debate started, to educate our neighbors, our friends and fellow citizens about the judicial tyranny that is corrupting American society and breeding a generation of ignorant, secular liberals. There is no advertising more effective than word of mouth. Just talk to your family, neighbors and friends about it in person, on the phone, and on the internet. Just imagine the impact of at least one simple yard sign on about every block in our cities, along country roads, and in practically all churches all over America. The central theme of those signs should be "Let the People be Free!"

In addition to yard signs (the size of a real estate 'For Sale' sign) cling signs for car windows, or bumper stickers, and magnetic car signs could add to the campaign. Warehouse businesses could post large signs on their buildings in industrial parks that are near major thoroughfares across the country. Restaurants could put messages on marquises or small tent signs on tables. Businesses of all sorts could show their patriotism in a number of creative ways. At the end of this chapter is a list of possible slogans and sign messages from which to select. Add your own creativity to come up with slogans of your own. For parades and yards homemade signs can be very effective because people know you cared enough to take pains to make a worthwhile statement.

COMMUNICATE ON THE INTERNET- <u>This is the best way to get the message out quickly and economically. We can grow</u>

quickly by using the internet to send e-mails alerting everyone on your address list. Make extensive use of all internet capabilities to communicate messages on websites and BLOGS to make an increasing number of our fellow Americans aware of the Revolution to Restore intelligent order to the judicial system in America and Revive our unalienable God-given rights. Websites and BLOGS communicate well. Start by going online to www.newpatriotsofamerica.org. The site is reachable also at .com and .net.

ORGANIZE YOUR CHURCH OR CIVIC GROUP- Talk up the New American Revolution for the Revival and Protection of our Rights to freedom of religion and freedom of speech at your church, synagogue or civic organization. Take up a collection for the printing of signs to be issued or purchased by the members, or distributed in neighborhoods, or wherever Americans want to stand up for justice and our rightful liberties. Every Church should get involved in this Great Revival and post a sign on their lawn or building that expresses their concern for protecting the free exercise of religion and freedom of speech as guaranteed by the Constitution. Don't do church signs that are leaning heavily toward a political message so as to avoid attacks by the ACLU before we get 'Separation of church and State' declared unconstitutional. Just keep it in the vein of standing up for our unalienable God-given rights as human beings. It might be best if entire large denominations would get together and do it all at once. If your church leadership doesn't have the courage to stand up and defend our right to freedom of religion in America, I suggest you should seek to attend a church that will. Christians need to get involved in the political process and even run for office, rather than run from it, because if we don't, the alternative is to be governed and ruled over by heathens who will enact laws contrary our religious values. John Jay, the first Supreme Court Chief Justice, was right when he stated we should choose Christians as our government leaders.

I would like to acknowledge and honor Dr. D. James Kennedy, founder of Coral Ridge Presbyterian Church in Fort Lauderdale, Florida, for also founding an outreach ministry known as the Center for Reclaiming America for Christ, headed by Dr. Gary Cass, who puts together a dynamic yearly Seminar with many prominent speakers, workshops, a banquet, displays and an inspirational musical grand finale. Coral Ridge Ministries has also established a lobby in Washington D.C. fighting to restore and protect our religious rights. Coral Ridge Ministries is leading the way as an excellent example of how churches should be involved in the political process to prevent subversion of our religious values by the forces of darkness.

God has the power to cut Satan down to size, and He will do it if today's people of God will wake up, repent and cast off their lukewarm complacent attitudes, stand up for God's righteousness and **do what Christ has commissioned Christians to do— pray and seek the face of God, ask for His righteousness to prevail in our lives, show a willingness to proclaim God's word to be the light of the world and the salt of the earth.** God promises in II Chronicles 7:14— "If My people who are called by My name will humble themselves, and pray and seek my face, and will turn from their wicked ways, then I will hear from heaven, and will forgive their sin and heal their land."

ORGANIZE RALLIES AND MARCHES- Get your patriotic religious rights or civic organization to stage rallies in stadiums, public parks or church properties. Also plan parades and marches both locally and in Washington D.C. Invite the press to these events and encourage them to capture the truth of your intentions to resurrect our most basic and sacred liberties, which were guaranteed by the Bill of Rights, until judges of bad behavior and incompetence on the Supreme Court and Circuit Courts began to take our rights away.

A major **Constitutional Reclamation and Revival of our Rights Convention** must be planned that will focus National attention on the New Patriots movement and will involve delegates from every State who will sign ***The New Patriots of America Declaration of Dependence on God.*** Delegates at this Convention will be allowed to discuss the wording and be able to make suggestions regarding additions or deletions to the document. Other activities at the convention might be a ceremonial burning of Darwin's book of lies, "The Origin of Species." Of course, there will be many speeches by prominent ministers, famous personalities and broadcasters who will inspire the nation with righteous rhetoric before a national radio and TV audience.

VOTE REPUBLICAN- How a person votes is a sacred, personal, private right. But remember, it is very important to give the President as much of a majority as possible in order to better secure Senate approval of changes with Supreme Court judges. So for the next few elections I want to encourage those people who want to get us back on the moral track to a better America to vote a straight Republican ticket. If enough votes are there to effect the necessary approval, perhaps it will cut down on the disgraceful circus the Democrat Party leadership displays on the Senate Judiciary Committee to satisfy their chosen base of special interest groups during the "advice and consent" debates.

In chapter 5 of this book I already pointed out how the Democrat Party leadership has been deceived and on the wrong side of the issues which are of concern to Values Voters. Let's pray they will see the light someday and stand up for what is truly right according to God's word, not what they declare to be politically correct according to those with worldly desires. However, to be realistic, we can't expect Democrats to change their stripes overnight since the Party Platform and the Party Base is made up of liberal principles and evil groups that support those wicked concepts. Beware of individual Democrat candidates who claim to be moderates with moral values. They are still under pressure by the Party to vote the liberal Party line once elected. A good example of this was revealed in the 2006 campaign of Democrat Senator Bob Casey who openly ran as a "pro-faith, pro life candidate" and yet one of his first admissions after being elected was that he planned to work with homosexuals to advance hate-crimes in the Senate. Some moderate family man he turned out to be. To be safe I urge Values Voters to vote Republican as long as GOP candidates uphold Godly principles the way Ronald Reagan did. He said, "The Good Lord who has given our country so much should never have been expelled from our nation's classrooms."

NEVER VOTE FOR A THIRD PARTY CANDIDATE- Third Party candidates rarely win elections, but they can determine who does win by swinging enough votes away from one or the other Democratic or Republican frontrunners. For example, people who voted for Ross Perot were responsible for pulling enough votes away from George Herbert Walker Bush in 1992 to get Bill Clinton elected by the electoral college even though Bush received the popular vote. Voting for a third Party candidate is not only a wasted vote, it's a good way to get the worst candidate elected to the White House. For the foreseeable future, I urge you to vote a straight Republican ticket. Especially the moderate Democrats, who might believe as Ronald Reagan, declared, "I didn't leave my party! My party left me." (He started as a Democrat.) If moderate Democrats would vote Republican, instead of not exercising their right to vote at all, it might get the liberal Democrats to come back to being more patriotic.

NEVER SPLIT YOUR VOTE- Splitting your vote between candidates of different parties to vote "for the man" is also a sure way to get a government that is stalemated on the issues, and nothing gets accomplished. Until recent times, Americans have had a tradition of deadlocking the government into partisan stalemates by voting for a President of one political party and giving him a congress dominated by the opposing party. Again, in order to get something accomplished to make changes for the better, vote a straight Republican ticket.

ENCOURAGE CHRISTIANS TO ENTER THE RACE- Our first Supreme Court Chief Justice, John Jay said we should prefer Christians as our rulers. To do otherwise is to be ruled by people who may not share our values, or be downright hostile to people of faith. There are many qualified Christian men and women who would make wonderful Senators and members of the House, as well as other government offices including Governors and, of course, the Presidency. Encourage people you know who would make good candidates for public office to get involved. Ask God if *you* are that person He would like to serve others and the nation in that capacity. After all, let's not fall victim to the Devil's plot of "separation of Church and State" to divide us from government and let us be ruled by the forces of darkness. It's very important for Christians to get involved in politics in order to preserve our values and America's heritage.

Actions to Avoid

It is very important that all actions taken to promote this movement be done with good taste and within the limits of the laws. Make certain proper permits are attained before staging parades or rallies. Display only signs and slogans that are in good taste. Don't use any foul or extreme language or thoughts in any advertising. Don't stage any activity that is illegal, or is an obstacle or an aggravating nuisance. Remember if you stand up for what is good, you'll have to stand against those who stand up for evil. Even though people who are deceived and full of the devil may taunt you, avoid contentious situations. Turn the other cheek and walk away from trouble.

Luke 21:17,18— And ye shall be hated of all men for my name's sake. But there shall not an hair of your head perish.

NPA Promotional Ideas

The main slogan for NPA yard signs should emphasize the idea of freedom for the people and freedom from government tyranny that interferes with our unalienable rights. Unalienable rights in a free society that is a democratic republic means your rights cannot be separated from you or taken away by anyone, including and especially, any department of the government. Therefore the **main theme for signs** to advertise this, and get people talking and discussing these issues, is simply the following— **Let the People be Free!**

This slogan should be the main theme behind all advertising and should be on all signs. Where other slogans are used the main theme of "Let the People be Free!" should appear in small print at the top or bottom of the sign. It can be accompanied by whatever tasteful slogan the creative minds of America can produce. Other possible slogan suggestions for signs and posters are listed here. I encourage you to use your imagination to express some more revolutionary ideas to reclaim our rights and morality.

Alternant NPA Signs

Freedom Yes! **Separation No!** Let the People be Free

Be Astute in The Truth **Deny the Lie** Let the People be Free

Abort Bad Judge's Jobs Let the People be Free

God is Real **Evolution Unreal** Let the People be Free

It's Judgment Day **For the bad Judges** Let the People be Free

Put Out-of-Order
Judges
Out of Office

Let the People be Free

Down With Devil Judges

Let the People be Free

Freedom of Religion
Is God's Will

Let the People be Free

Freedom of Religion is
God's Plan for Man

Let the People be Free

Feel free to dream up your own ideas for other slogans to show support for this worthy cause to wage a Revolution for the Revival of our sacred rights.

-0-

The Spiritual Clock is Ticking

We must be aware of the spiritual clock that is ticking down to the return of Jesus Christ. In fact, there is something spiritual about the fact that God has inspired me to write this book, not because I am some kind of prophet or holy saint-like person. I'm not! It wasn't fully my idea. I'm just a very ordinary sinner as I said at the very beginning of this book. I have many weaknesses, faults and imperfections, to which anyone who knows me can testify. But, if God only worked with perfect people, He wouldn't have anyone to work His will through, because the Apostle Paul says all have sinned and fallen short of the glory of God. Even so, I'm still a bit awed that God gave me the title of this book. **The title of this book is not just God proclaiming His judgment of the courts, it is His condemnation of Satan's plans to corrupt America from within.**

God also gave me ideas about what to put in this book and how to format it. I had doubts about writing it, and when I asked God for a definite sign to verify He wanted me to write it, He miraculously showed me a huge, perfectly-shaped cross, cut out of the clouds of a totally overcast night sky, and He held it perfectly still for an unusually long period of time, directly in front of me, for as long as I needed to gaze at it to strengthen my faith in this mission. I have no doubt it was a miraculous communication and an absolute confirmation that He wanted me to write this book. It has not been easy to write, and I have been tempted to abandon this project many times, but I can't get the image and message of that cross out of my mind. Those who have a heart for God will harken to heed and champion the ideals set forth in this book, and those who have a heart for Satan will harden their hearts to challenge these ideals.

This book is not just about my desires. To God be the glory for what He reveals to us. He is a loving God, a merciful God. It is His will that not one should perish, but He is a pure God and an all-knowing God who tells us that, "wide is the way that leads to destruction. Straight and narrow is the path that leads to heaven, and few are they that find it." **God wants today's modern church to repent from our lukewarm ways and get hot for the truth of God that sets us free.** We are more wealthy than any generation in history, and have too many distractions and worldly interests that take our focus off of what is really important— eternal life! Because we own, or want to own, many worldly things, we feel we have need of nothing much, and we don't realize how spiritually wretched we are. We're spiritually miserable because we are storing up treasure for this life which we will shortly leave behind. We are spiritually poor because we're NOT storing up treasures in heaven by striving with enough conviction to deeply love God with great devotion, putting Him first in our lives and upholding His righteous virtues in order to honor and glorify God. We are spiritually blind and don't see we are mentally focused on short term goals. Our modern day attitudes make us lovers of pleasure more than lovers of the God who gave us life. We have become lukewarm and complacent in our worship of the Lord, which leaves us spiritually naked before Him. Too many people go to church and live the world's way the rest of the week.

Lukewarm Christians are so distasteful to Jesus, it makes Him want to throw up. That's what He means when He says in the book of Revelation (3:16) that He will spew us out of His mouth. After all, He loves us so much He was willing to suffer immensely and die for us! How many of us today are willing to be that totally committed to Him? What are our priorities? Do we really treasure His love and devotion to us enough? Or is our daily goal to seek earthly pleasures and get richer in the things of this world? Are such things as career ambitions, sports, entertainment, possessions, hobbies, all manner of worldly distractions and pleasures, even our loved ones, occupying our minds and hearts more than God and His glorious Kingdom? How foolish of us! Doesn't God indicate we can't even conceive of the things He has stored up for those who love Him? And the blessings God wants to bestow upon those who love Him are not something temporary. His blessings last forever! World without end, forever, forever, forever and forevermore throughout all eternity. Wonderful things we can not even imagine are awaiting those who love God. Are we going to be foolish enough to concentrate our desires on the immediate gratification of some worldly desires, gains, goals or pleasures we must surely give up upon death? Are we foolish enough to act like whatever we accomplish or accumulate in this life is really worth anything, since it will be short lived? Are we foolish enough to focus on the short term and miss the long term joys of eternal life in a heavenly atmosphere?

The return of Christ is rapidly approaching. No one knows the hour or the day, but signs of the season are popping up everywhere. We are like the seventh church that Christ described to John in Chapter three of the book of Revelation. And though His truthful view of us reveals us to be spoiled by the things of this modern world, Jesus still compassionately says in Rev. 3:18,19, "I counsel thee to buy of me gold tried in the fire, that thou mayest be rich; and white raiment, that thou mayest be clothed, and that the shame of thy nakedness do not appear; and anoint thine eyes with eyesalve, that thou mayest see. As many as I love, I rebuke and chasten; be zealous therefore and repent."

If it were not possible for us to repent, change and turn from our half-hearted, complacent, lukewarm ways, would He ask us to repent? Jesus is asking the generations of this age to get involved and be tried in the heated fight for righteousness which is as spiritual gold, and truly is worth something that will make us spiritually rich by storing up eternal treasure in heaven. He is asking us to clothe ourselves in the purity of His truth and love, and let the glory of acknowledging and worshipping Jesus Christ shine for all the darkened world to see the enlightenment of His ways. He is rebuking us and chastising us because He loves us and wants to see us repent from our spiritual mediocrity in order to bring about a great revolution, and fight for our right to freedom of religion, and our right to freedom of speech. He wants us to exercise that free speech to cause a great Spiritual Revival before the sound of the trump that will take us away from the dreadful tribulation. He is a God whose loving kindness endures forever. It is His will that not one should perish, even though the majority will miss it. But, if only one percent of the population of America gets saved by this movement to restore honoring God in school classrooms, government podiums, and all social atmospheres, that would be three million people. If there is great rejoicing over one who gets saved, how much more joy will there be over three million? This is an enormously worthwhile cause.

Must I remind you? LET'S GET BUSY! There is a great work to be done for God, and being busy for God is important in these end times before the return of Christ. You don't have to give up everything you enjoy. Much can be accomplished if you spend just a little bit of your time on this cause. Get busy and let your light shine in these days. Communicate your desire for freedom of religion to our government leaders. Don't be like the foolish virgins spoken of in Matthew 25 who neglected to get oil for their lamps and missed the coming of the bridegroom. And He told them, "I know you not." LET'S GET BUSY! Getting America back on track by ridding the Supreme Court of the devil's Judges will lay a foundation for a great end time Revival to take place in America and spread across the world. God bless those who participate.

Some people will read these things and will be offended and rebel against it. Still others will think it is too preachy, too religious, too Christian. Pray for these people, for they are either among the deceived of Satan, or are of a belief other than Christian, or are among the complacent, lukewarm Christians who are offended by a total commitment to God. Many Christians may say, "Why should I get involved? I believe rightly. I don't agree with the idea of separation of church and state, or believe in evolution, or abortion or homosexuality so why should I care what others do? It's none of my business! I'm not a party to their sins!" <u>Christians need to be concerned about the sins of others because God will hold us responsible for those we don't warn about evil.</u> This message is crystal clear as God speaks His word to the prophet, Ezekiel (33:8,9) "If I announce that some wicked people are sure to die and you fail to tell them to change their ways, then they will die in their sins, and I will hold you responsible for their deaths. But if you warn them to repent and they don't repent, they will die in their sins, but you will have saved yourself." Furthermore if the whole of American society, and the laws of government literally protect evil and reject God, (which is happening now) the time will come when the wrath of God will suddenly fall on the just and the unjust. The events of 9/11, the hurricanes in Florida in 2004 and those in the Gulf of 2005 and other disasters are warnings we are losing the blessings and protections of God.

We should NOT be ashamed of the gospel of Jesus Christ. Gospel means "good news," and there is no greater news than to be entitled to everlasting life by the simple act of faith in Jesus Christ, the only begotten Son of God! Pray for those who can't acknowledge Jesus Christ as their personal Savior because they may be ignorant of the fact our Lord Jesus humbled himself to suffer greatly and die to become the most holy sacrifice to ransom us and take away the sins of the world. I would like to remind the lukewarm Christians that if Christ was willing to suffer and die for you, why can't you at least stand up and be brave enough to demand that your right to believe as you see fit should not be compromised? To those of other faiths, I want to point out that the Judeo-Christian heritage of America is no threat to you in any way, because Christians do not war against you or condemn you. We only hope to offer you the joy of salvation and eternal life in a heavenly place. Christianity is only for those who are willing to accept Jesus by their own free will. And to those of the Jewish faith, I want to say you are very special to the true Christians, who are your greatest spiritual friends outside of your faith. We recognize and respect the fact that Judaism is the very foundation from which Christianity grew. Even though we have differences of belief, never underestimate the love of Christians for Jews whom we recognize as God's chosen people. The age of the gentiles is drawing to a close, and the day of the Jews is drawing near as God alone will gloriously intervene to save the Jewish nation.

The Founding Fathers of America encouraged, and even personally promoted Christianity, but left the wording of the Bill of Rights open to complete religious freedom of the people to believe and express their beliefs, with no one being forced to worship or believe any certain way, or forced to be deprived of freedom of worship or beliefs by governmental dictates. The purpose and intent of the New Patriots of America allows for, and upholds complete freedom of religion, freedom of beliefs and opinions for all Americans, with no one being forced to accept, worship or believe anything other than the true desires of their hearts and souls. Freedom is the will of God. He wants people to be free to exercise the gift of their own free will. He wants us to freely choose which side we want to be on. He lays before us life and death, blessings and curses, and our fate is our own choice.

So, where are we on the spiritual clock? What is the sequence of events that will be played out before us in the immediate and near future? I will only summarize a general overview, but if you want more detailed information about the prophecies relating to the end-times I suggest you investigate the writings, recordings, web-sites and ministries of such apocalyptic icons as John Hagee, Perry Stone, Jack Van Impe, Rod Parsley, David Reagan and Hal Lindsey, to name a few. As far as the common denominator basics of end-time prophecies go, Judeo-Christian scriptures indicate that there will be a seven year rule by an individual described as the antichrist. Three and a half years (or 42 months) into his reign of terror he will actually declare himself to be God and demand the whole world, that is held hostage under his control, to worship him as Lord. This time is described by Jesus Christ as the worst of times that ever have been or will ever be again. During this evil dominance of the peoples of the earth, Christians and Jews will be persecuted for their beliefs. But, at the end of the seven year reign of this tyrant and his talking beast, Jesus Christ will return to the earth to destroy the antichrist and his armies, which will have gathered to overthrow and conquer Israel in the Battle of Armageddon.

However, prior to all of this taking place, Bible scriptures and the Apostle Paul prophesy of an event that modern-day evangelistic ministers often refer to as, "the rapture of the church." Because the Bible makes no mention of the word 'rapture,' many people have doubts about it. Don't get hung up or confused about the word 'rapture.' The event, also known as 'the snatching away of the church,' **is going to take place just as prophesied** in I Thessalonians 4: 16-18, "For the Lord Himself will descend from heaven with a shout, with the voice of an archangel, and with the trumpet of God. And the dead in Christ will rise first. Then we who are alive and remain shall be caught up together with them in the clouds to meet the Lord in the air; And thus we shall always be with the Lord. Therefore comfort one another with these words." This is how Christ is going to allow His most faithful followers to escape the horrors of the tribulation. In Luke 21:36 He warns, "Watch ye therefore, and pray always, that ye may be accounted worthy to escape all these things that shall come to pass, and to stand before the Son of Man."

Before the tribulation and the rapture of the faithful takes place, doesn't it make sense that our Lord, who is a merciful God and desires that not one should perish, would want to prepare as many good-hearted but lost souls as possible to be saved? I urge all dear hearts to forget about the foolish cares of this world, and the short life we are living, and concentrate on the long-term goal of eternal life and endless joy. Do what Christ has asked of the Laodicean church age generation. (That's us, today!) Repent! Change! Turn around and embrace God's perfect ways! Buy of

Him gold tried in the fire of an end-of-age Revolution for the Revival of our rights to freedom of religion, freedom of speech, and the protection of freedom of the press (The Holy Bible) from those deceived and disoriented servants of Satan who would love to have the Bible banned as a "hate book."

Christians need to unite, forget our petty differences, and even join with people of other faiths who are willing to fight for the Revival of our original rights to believe as we see fit, and to freely express our beliefs, because **the whole concept of freedom of religion is under attack by a tyrannical judicial department of government.** Wake up America! This is NOT just a cultural war. It's NOT a battle of the radical right against the radical left. It's not Democrats against Republicans. It's not the East Against the West. It's not Islam against Jews and Christians and all other religions. It's a battle of wrong against right! **We're in a Spiritual War!** We battle NOT against our brothers and sisters in the flesh. We battle against those who are deceived by Satan. **It's Satan against God!** This spiritual war has been raging for thousands of years involving every human being who ever drew breath, and the final battles will be fought in the next few years.

We've all seen videos of a small devil on the shoulder of a man, and a good angel on the other, both trying to influence the man regarding good or evil. Although that is a somewhat amusing image, it is not far from the truth of real life. Demons and good angels are out there. They are around all of us, and they do tempt us, influencing our feelings and our thinking. Even though our mortal eyes can't see it, **the spiritual world is real**! And the **Spiritual War is real! We need to get real and face the truth of it.**

Who would have thought that God-loving, God-fearing Americans would have to fight a second American Revolution to revive the same unalienable rights that our Founding Fathers fought and died for us to inherit? Let's enlist ourselves in the great latter days Army of God, The New Patriots of America, and get involved in the Revolution to be victorious in the battles for a Revival of freedom and the salvation of many souls. Let's re-align our priorities, put aside the fruitless desires and actions of this limited worldly life, and take up the gauntlet to fight for the ageless values and principles of Almighty God. Our weapons are prayer, devout faith, truth and love. We only need a few good men and women to get this movement started. Are you up to the challenge to inspire our leaders, and the President, to act on our behalf to restore America as truly the land of responsible free people? Are you brave enough to stand up for what is eternally right? If you are, then together with others like you, with certainty we can truly claim America as the land of the free and the home of the brave!

Let the Revolution Begin! And Let the People be Free!

The End…

…of this book is the beginning of the Revival of our most sacred rights and values!

PRAY! And trust God for the Victory.

Psalms 33:12— Blessed is the nation whose God is the Lord, The people He has chosen as His own inheritance.

Isaiah 54:17— No weapon that is formed against thee shall prosper; and every tongue that shall rise against thee in judgment thou shalt condemn. This is the heritage of the servants of the Lord, and their righteousness is of me, saith the Lord.

Proverbs 14:34— Righteousness exalts a nation: but sin is a reproach to any people.

Made in the USA
Monee, IL
08 November 2026

67380515R00098